# Raising the Bar Mitzvah

# Raising the Bar Mitzvah

*Reimagining What Our Kids Learn*

Cantor Matt Axelrod

**ROWMAN & LITTLEFIELD**
Lanham • Boulder • New York • London

Published by Rowman & Littlefield
An imprint of The Rowman & Littlefield Publishing Group, Inc.
4501 Forbes Boulevard, Suite 200, Lanham, Maryland 20706
www.rowman.com

6 Tinworth Street, London SE11 5AL, United Kingdom

British Library Cataloguing in Publication Information Available

**Library of Congress Cataloging-in-Publication Data**

Names: Axelrod, Matt, 1966– author.
Title: Raising the bar mitzvah : reimagining what our kids learn / Cantor Matt Axelrod.
Description: Lanham : Rowman & Littlefield, [2021] | Includes bibliographical
   references and index.
Identifiers: LCCN 2020013405 (print) | LCCN 2020013406 (ebook) | ISBN
   9781538133088 (cloth) | ISBN 9781538133095 (paperback) | ISBN
   9781538133101 (epub)
Subjects: LCSH: Bar mitzvah. | Bat mitzvah.
Classification: LCC BM707 .A938 2020  (print) | LCC BM707  (ebook) | DDC
   296.424—dc23
LC record available at https://lccn.loc.gov/2020013405
LC ebook record available at https://lccn.loc.gov/2020013406

For my parents of blessed memory,
Muriel and Saul Axelrod ז״ל


*Train up a child in the way he should go,*
*and when he is old he will not depart from it.*
Proverbs 22:6

# Contents

# Preface

## *Everything Has Already Changed*

There were many things that I expected after I came up with the concept for this book and wrote *Raising the Bar Mitzvah*. I assumed that there would be a great deal of pushback and resistance to a lot of the ideas that I was bring- ing up. As you'll read in great detail, our current system of celebrating b'nei mitzvah ceremonies has remained largely unchanged for generations. Over the past decades, we have been training kids the same way, while expecting them to meet the identical requirements as their parents and grandparents did before them. Furthermore, all of the stakeholders in this process— parents, kids, and of course Jewish professionals—are utterly invested in this model. The idea of change is understandably threatening—for emotional, religious, and financial reasons.

While I have always hoped that my book might serve as an eye-opening catalyst for change, or at the very least as some food for thought that could be discussed over the kitchen counter or conference room table at a synagogue ritual committee meeting, I did not figure that Jewish life would make a sud- den tectonic shift away from the status quo of how we prepare kids for b'nei mitzvah. Rather, if my book can be part of a larger conversation about and evaluation of what we do and how we do it, then I'd consider that a success.

What I could not possibly have foreseen while I was writing this book was a global pandemic.

This unprecedented turn of events has not only affected every measure of our daily routines, but has wholly altered Jewish life as well. As I write this preface, a huge percentage of the Jewish community has not set foot in a synagogue in months. Services are being livestreamed. Committees are meeting via video conferencing. There are no handshakes, kiddush lunches, or noisy children in Hebrew school classrooms. B'nei mitzvah lessons, much like the rest of children's education, now take place remotely. Plexiglass barriers have been installed in temple offices and on bimah podiums.

And suddenly all b'nei mitzvah services have undergone a profound transformation as well. In a bizarre turn of events, the pandemic's effects have resulted in a number of changes that reflect the very rethinking and reimagining that I have suggested in the chapters that follow.

In the beginning stages of this crisis, most people did not anticipate its duration or severity. Our local governments issued regulations that meant that for the time being, we could not gather in person in public locations, including the temple sanctuary. The term "social distancing" was still a novelty at that time. So how did that affect the myriad families who had b'nei mitzvah services and parties scheduled for the spring—usually the busiest time of year for these events?

Families faced two major options:

- Have the bar or bat mitzvah as scheduled—virtually, with whatever technical arrangements their synagogue was capable of setting up. Then postpone the actual reception to a later date, which was often the most complicated part of the process because most reception locations are booked more than a year in advance.
- Postpone everything until later in the year, when the entire crisis would presumably have passed. This meant finding an available alternate date both on the temple calendar and at the party venue.

Having now officiated at numerous virtual b'nei mitzvah services, I, along with many cantorial and rabbinical colleagues, have been amazed at the results. It's as if we've been able to stage a global experiment involving b'nei mitzvah kids and parents. These are some of the basic questions that these forced conditions have brought to the fore—and the very same questions that I bring up throughout this book:

- What are the most important aspects of becoming bar or bat mitzvah?
- What is the real connection of the lavish party or reception to the religious ceremony?
- Who is the intended audience of the b'nei mitzvah service?
- What are your goals (or those of your child, student, or bar or bat mitzvah family)?

And the overarching question became this:

- How has your understanding of what it means to become b'nei mitzvah changed since the COVID-19 pandemic began?

For those families who opted to proceed with the ceremony as scheduled, that meant juggling the child's participation, the family's presence, and finding a way to include the smaller circle of close relatives and friends along with the much larger circle of everyone else they would normally have invited to be present in the sanctuary. One way that a number of synagogues balanced these needs was to utilize a hybrid of video conferencing (the most popular platform has been Zoom), which would then be livestreamed to the congregation and larger group of guests (often via Facebook or YouTube).

### As an Aside . . .

Any of these virtual options are only available to those synagogues that have made the decision to utilize this technology on Shabbat. During normal times, some Conservative synagogues had already been livestreaming services via a static installed webcam. Others chose not to do so because the rabbi and religious leadership deemed that to be a violation of Shabbat restrictions.

It's fascinating to note that the Committee on Jewish Laws and Standards that rules on *halachah*—Jewish law—for the Conservative Movement issued a number of rulings that made allowances for the use of technology like this for Shabbat services under certain conditions. It was still dependent on the decision of the individual congregation, but they correctly and sensibly recognized that the Jewish community needed a way—any way—to gather as a congregation and find a way to connect religiously and spiritually during these exigent circumstances.

Within numerous congregations, the results were striking and surprising. In many cases, the families converted their "Zoom Room" into a makeshift mini-sanctuary, often decorated with a beautiful tablecloth, ritual items, and flowers. Family members eschewed the stiff and uncomfortable new suit or dress and opted instead for more comfortable and less formal (but still appropriate) attire. Relatives and friends, via Zoom, were present and ironically felt *closer* to the action than if they had been sitting far removed in sanctuary pews.

Families and synagogues have been left with a scaled-down and bare-bones version of what they thought a bar or bat mitzvah ceremony would look like. The key elements of what typical families wanted—marking a threshold in time, celebrating an accomplishment, observing a ritual within the context of the larger community—are all present. But other routine aspects of the occasion are now absent. There is no longer a feeling that this service is a pageant. People are not present in services dressed in party attire. Less has become more. And rather than feel that circumstances have robbed them of a once-in-a-lifetime experience, b'nei mitzvah families have walked away with a feeling of joy and spirituality.

Our enforced experiment to change the way we think about celebrating the bar or bat mitzvah has been a success.

There is one question that has not yet been answered because we don't yet know when distancing regulations will be lifted: What will happen with the bar or bat mitzvah party? For the families that postponed the reception until some future date, their celebration will now be detached from the religious piece. Later in this book, I look closely at some of the more problematic aspects of what has become a typical bar or bat mitzvah celebration. Will that still be the case if the party comes a year after the service, rather than hours after?

We all pray for the day when we can resume life as normal. We mourn the suffering of those affected by COVID-19. My greatest hope is that by the time you read these words, this pandemic and all of the changes that it has brought will be relegated to memory as something that happened in the past and that we can't believe ever happened or that we made it through. But there's no denying that its effects have already engendered a rethinking of b'nei mitzvah that matches many of the points that you will read throughout the coming chapters.

Let's now continue to rethink how we train our kids and what we expect from them—and start to reimagine what our kids learn.

~

# Introduction

## *Let's Reimagine the Possibilities*

What was your bar or bat mitzvah like?

Let me see if I can guess, regardless of whether you now make your living as a Jewish professional or belong to a congregation of any size:

A few years or so before the big day, your family was assigned a date by your synagogue. This date was based on your Hebrew birthday, with the temple trying to schedule your bar or bat mitzvah as close to your thirteenth birthday as possible.

A few conscientious parents figured out which Torah portion fell on that future weekend (no small feat in pre-Internet days), and if you got one of the less-desirable passages (leprosy, forbidden intimate relationships—okay, anything in Leviticus), then they started negotiating with the temple to reschedule the date to something more interesting (anything featured in the *Ten Commandments* movie that everyone watched each year).

With the date firmly established on the calendar, it was time to start planning. In addition to the myriad details involved in the party (venue, food, music, invitations), you had to begin the dreaded bar or bat mitzvah lessons at temple. These sessions, whether thirty, forty-five, or sixty minutes a week, would involve meeting with the cantor, rabbi, or other tutor in order to learn a bunch of material.

And what did you have to learn?

While some of the specifics might differ among various individuals, the one likely constant, and certainly the most daunting, was the hafto-rah (or *haftarah*, which, we'll discover later on, better reflects the Hebrew pronunciation, and which I will use throughout the rest of this book). This mysterious multipage text was presented to you in a booklet or folder that you were expected to keep safe and bring to every lesson. It was written in a distinctive font that made it look vaguely holy—so you knew this was serious business. Most of the lessons consisted of the cantor trying to teach you indecipherable trope accents—small shapes or symbols that appear on each word that determine how to sing the text. You were expected to memorize these tunes by using the recording that the cantor gave you to take home. You can map out the distinct generations of twentieth-century Jewish history by dividing up the cutting-edge technologies of the day—reel-to-reel tape (well before my time), cassette tapes, CDs, or MP3s. (Will VR or holograms make it into a future edition of this book?)

Regardless of how long ago your bar or bat mitzvah took place, I predict that you can still sing the first few words of your haftarah from memory. And then everything goes blank.

Depending on how well you sing, your musical background, how well you read Hebrew, and maybe how often your family attended services, you either had a relatively easy time memorizing your way through the haftarah or it was a multimonth period of drama and agony, with your parents fighting with you to practice. Either way, when your bar or bat mitzvah day finally arrived, somehow you did manage to get through the haftarah.

Don't forget about the speech. As part of lessons, you met with the rabbi to discuss your Torah portion. This would form the basis for your speech, where you talked about what took place in the Torah that week (and this is where you hope you didn't get the part about incestuous relationships). Your speech ended with thanking your little brother for not annoying you while you were trying to practice and then, finally, your parents for everything that they did to prepare you for this big day. If you had even a little more poise than the average thirteen-year-old kid, you didn't read the whole thing in one breath and you remembered to look up at least once.

I predict that no matter how old you are, where you grew up, or what your temple was like, this was at least a fairly accurate description of your bar or bat mitzvah experience.

In fact, there are numerous other aspects of the experience that could be quite different depending on your location or background:

- Were women allowed to participate in the service?
- Was a bat mitzvah service identical to that of a bar mitzvah or were there alternate requirements for girls?

- Were there non-Jewish members of the family present or involved in the service?
- Did the liturgy—the words of the siddur, or prayer book—reflect more modern theological concepts or was it strictly the traditional text?
- Was your rabbi or cantor male or female?

The answers to all of these questions would vary greatly depending on when your bar or bat mitzvah took place. Readers who came of age in the 1960s or 1970s would give completely different responses to these questions than their counterparts of the 1990s or 2000s. That's because so much has changed in Jewish life in a relatively short time.

In many communities, irrespective of denomination, the congregation is entirely egalitarian, treating men and women, boys and girls as completely equal participants. That means all bar or bat mitzvah preparation, participation in the service, presence on the bimah, and involvement in synagogue leadership is open to all.

Interfaith marriage is still a difficult subject for many, and while various temples deal with this part of modern Jewish life in assorted ways, there's no getting around the fact that a significant number of Jewish families contain non-Jewish members. Whether they would be allowed to participate or be present on the bimah at all would likely vary considerably.

*But the one constant—transcending each generation, trend, social movement, or religious level—is how we prepare b'nei mitzvah kids and what we teach them.*

Among all the sweeping changes that have taken place, the bar or bat mitzvah experience has gone mostly unchanged over the last decades. Put another way: this *is* your father's bar mitzvah. In fact, this is your grandfather's bar mitzvah. We are still turning out Jews who have been trained using a model from the 1940s.

We emphasize synagogue skills, drill rote memorization, and require singing from every kid regardless of aptitude, talent, ability, interest, maturity, or personality. There may be a passing effort at some critical thought and a token requirement for a community service project of some kind, but the main focus by far is on memorizing a set of texts and reciting them in front of a group of invited guests.

So if the preparation is exactly the same, it comes as no surprise that when the bar or bat mitzvah is over, most kids walk away with the identical result. They got through it (and yes, usually quite well) but will likely not use a lot of those skills again. It sounds a lot like how many of you remember algebra.

I've painted a pretty bleak picture of this aspect of the American Jewish experience. Of course, it's not all terrible.

Some of our kids are in fact extremely well served by this largely unchanged model of b'nei mitzvah preparation. These individuals possess a strong talent for Hebrew reading or music and excel at chanting the words. Their families are regular and active members of the congregation, and they are likely to be present at many future services and will participate again—maybe chanting another haftarah or Torah reading.

And even for those kids and families that exist on the margins of Jewish life, preparing for a bar or bat mitzvah and participating in the service is a powerful way to identify with the Jewish community and make a bold statement. Certainly the period leading up to and then culminating in a bar or bat mitzvah has marked the first time a previously uninvolved family has been inspired to re-evaluate their connection to tradition and their congregation.

Even so, we can do better. More importantly, we *have* to do better.

Bar and bat mitzvah preparation should not be a one-size-fits-all process.

What would happen if we completely reimagined what our children's b'nei mitzvah looked like? How would you react if I came up to you and said, "Forget everything you know about a bar or bat mitzvah. You now get to reinvent the whole thing from scratch"?

First, there would be some questions that you'd have to answer:

- What will the student learn?
- What are we trying to accomplish?
- What is the goal of the bar or bat mitzvah?
- At what age should this take place? (If we're reimagining, who says it has to be thirteen?)
- Should there be a service?
- Do we need to belong to a temple?

I find that once you start posing these questions, it's hard to stop. If you put everything on the table for discussion, then you can stop assuming that the bar or bat mitzvah must look and feel one exact way.

And this is the most important underlying question of all and the theme that will drive each word of this book:

*If all of our kids are individuals, with various abilities and specific interests, why are we insisting on one immutable model of Jewish learning?*

And the answer, of course, is that it doesn't have to be that way. It's time to stop preparing yet another generation of modern Jews using the education and goals of decades past. "Just because we've always done it this way" is not a good reason to avoid challenging the status quo.

To be sure, there are certainly existing opportunities already for individual families to seek out significantly varied models of training for and celebrating b'nei mitzvah. Numerous independent clergy, tutors, or officiants are more than willing to encourage a wide range of options to tailor the bar or bat mitzvah experience to a family's individual needs. Many congregational clergy are also cognizant of the limitations of the existing model and make a dedicated and concerted effort to vary the process as needed for a meaningful, spiritual, and educational outcome.

But read that last paragraph again. By using terms such as "vary the process" and "tailor the experience," we're implying that there is one de facto, accepted model and path, and we should recognize the few brave souls who have attempted to swim against the current (which we definitely should). A good number of Jewish professionals will read the words of this book and respond with some version of "But I already do a lot of these things." In many ways, this is a classic definition of the exception proving the rule.

Let's look closely at how we got here. We need to understand the context of current b'nei mitzvah training and why we seem to be stuck with this particular model. But then we'll look at some fascinating possibilities, combining traditional aspects of training with brand-new ideas. Our current process does benefit one type of student very well. But when we utterly reimagine everything we know, then every child—regardless of specific skills, ability, or background—will not only excel but will also find tremendous meaning in becoming bar or bat mitzvah.

It's hard to transform a system that has become solidly entrenched. My goal is to inspire changes that are both practical and modest, as well as wildly ambitious steps to reimagine the entire notion of what it means to become b'nei mitzvah and to mark that milestone. Throughout the text, you'll see boxes entitled "Raising the Bar" that will identify ways that both professionals and congregants can enhance what our kids learn and make the material more relevant and accessible. These boxes represent possible first steps that could be undertaken by many individuals and synagogues without drastically upending all that is familiar to Jewish communities. I've also included other boxes entitled "As an Aside . . . " to further explain or amplify some ideas or concepts that will enhance one's understanding.

This is a process and, therefore, this book is intended for both the Jewish professional world of synagogue leaders and b'nei mitzvah teachers, as well as parents who are seeking to make the very best decisions for their children's Jewish development. Whether you're able to completely revamp the process from the ground up or make incremental changes, we can start thinking about how to adapt and modify the way we've been doing things over the past century.

So let's begin a conversation. Unlike in other areas of Jewish life, this will be a completely judgment-free zone. Too often, some Jews live on the margins of Jewish or congregational life because they are made to feel inferior for not observing a certain way or for not knowing a set of facts that "everyone else" knows. And pity the poor parents who have the gall to suggest that they don't wish to proceed with their child's bar or bat mitzvah, either right now or for the foreseeable future, because of any number of reasons—educational, financial, social, religious, or spiritual. They feel deep down that something is missing but are not able (or even more likely, not allowed) to articulate how it could be different. This book will give voice to those parents, as well as to all of my fellow Jewish professionals—clergy, educational directors, teachers, and b'nei mitzvah tutors—who struggle to teach one traditional set of materials, text, and melodies to every single child.

For the next thirteen chapters, you are *encouraged* to challenge, ask, opine, and disrupt. Reimagine embarking on what should be a journey leading toward maturity and adulthood in a way that differs—either slightly or profoundly—from the path that everyone else seems to be happily and passively taking. We owe it to ourselves and our kids to give them every opportunity to connect with Judaism and relate to their tradition on an adult level in the most meaningful way possible.

PART I

~

# WHERE WE'VE BEEN

# CHAPTER ONE

~

# The History

Nobody gets *bar mitzvahed*.

Perhaps the biggest misconception that exists throughout all reaches of Jewish life is that having a bar or bat mitzvah changes a young person. Before the special day, this thirteen-year-old child is walking around with the status of a minor. Then they lead some parts of the service, chant (or struggle) their way through a haftarah, receive a blessing from the rabbi and some tearful words from their parents, and—suddenly—they are now bar mitzvahed! From this point forward, they are Jewish adults, although whatever privileges that entails are not usually made clear. For instance, they still have to attend Religious School in the afternoon.

The reality might surprise you.

First, the term bar or bat mitzvah is used as an adjective. It's not a thing that happens or a process that changes a person. It simply signifies that an individual is now old enough, within the framework of Jewish law and tradition, to be able to participate in certain activities reserved for adults. These include being counted in a minyan—the minimum quorum of ten individuals needed for certain prayers in a service—and being able to lead these services if called upon.

There's no ceremony that *makes* this happen. It's automatic the moment a Jewish kid turns thirteen. Like someone who is eligible to vote when they turn eighteen or drink an alcoholic beverage upon turning twenty-one, it just happens. No one needs to do a thing; the child takes on a new status simply by virtue of being a certain age.

Many of us who lead congregations come across older Jewish women—typically from a generation past when girls did not regularly celebrate a bat mitzvah at all—who are now afraid to accept any honor in the service because they "were never bat mitzvahed." Since it's fairly obvious that these women are old enough to be considered Jewish adults, this argument doesn't make any sense. The unfortunate part is that they've gone their whole lives feeling religiously inferior—not worthy or eligible to participate fully in Jewish life and ritual—because of a fundamental misunderstanding of Jewish tradition.

As we'll see, properly understood, the bar or bat mitzvah ceremony is not a process but rather a commemoration of something that has already happened. Anyone is free to celebrate the fact, ignore it, choose not to belong to a synagogue, reject every facet of Judaism, or any other possible action. But unless a person knows how to stop time, every Jewish child becomes bar or bat mitzvah as soon as they pass their thirteenth birthday. Motivation, education, and preparation don't enter into that immutable fact.

## Why Thirteen?

A better question might be, why *not* thirteen? Even though this might be one of the most common, ingrained pieces of Jewish life that exists, there is actually no specific prescription within *halacha*, Jewish law, that mandates that the age of maturity must be age thirteen. It has certainly been passed down orally throughout the generations and enjoys the status of what I might call folk-halacha. Its origin can be traced back to Talmudic times when the rabbis, somewhat arbitrarily, decided that this was the age when a typical boy went through puberty.

### As an Aside . . .

And to get further in the weeds, there are certain physical criteria that the rabbis identified that would determine whether the boy had in fact entered puberty, some of which border on cringeworthy. If the boy didn't demonstrate these characteristics, he would not be considered eligible for a bar mitzvah. Pity the poor late-blooming kids. I suppose this alone might constitute a fairly sensible rationale for instituting one age for everyone.

Even though all boys, as any bar mitzvah tutor or middle-school teacher knows, begin and progress through puberty at all different times, we have stuck firmly to the unalterable age of thirteen as the threshold. You are a child on *that* side, but an adult on *this* side. Any indications of ability, maturity, intelligence, emotional capacity, or even willingness to accept an added set of responsibilities have been deemed irrelevant.

Then we come to the much more complicated subject of girls and how they have been treated within Jewish ritual throughout history. It's difficult to trace the origin of the required age for bat mitzvah girls for the simple reason that traditionally this never applied to them. Historically this was something reserved only for males. Girls were never considered part of this process because, according to strict Jewish tradition, girls and women were never required to take on these roles at all. All post–bar mitzvah privileges—being counted in a minyan, taking part in a service, receiving honors to the Torah—were closed to all women regardless of age.

### As an Aside . . .

While we might consider this treatment of women and girls to be an anachronistic reading of halachic Judaism, this likely made more sense in past generations. Jewish law exempted women from what were referred to as "time-bound commandments"—that is, responsibilities that had to be performed at a specific time in a particular place. The assumption was that women were burdened with taking care of the home and the children and thus were not free to drop everything and get themselves to a place of worship. As most in the non-Orthodox world would agree, this does not present a compelling argument in more modern and egalitarian times and is thankfully not the common practice in most Jewish communities.

The journey to create a comparable experience for girls has taken a more convoluted path. Rather than simply say that girls will reach the age of maturity at thirteen along with their male counterparts, it was decided that the age of twelve would be a more logical choice. If we are in fact looking to the criteria of going through puberty to be the deciding factor, then it's clear that girls mature, both physically and emotionally, at a somewhat earlier age than boys. Even a quick glance at a seventh-grade class bears this out, with most of the girls towering over their hapless male classmates.

As a result, even today, there is still no one accepted age that is the definitive point at which a girl has a bat mitzvah. Instead, it's usually left up to the individual synagogue's policies on how they distribute dates. Some simply take all the kids in the same class and consider that the b'nei mitzvah class, while others will make a distinction between when the boys turn thirteen and the girls turn twelve.

But regardless of the specific procedures of a given Jewish community, the age of Jewish maturity at thirteen is virtually universal. Later on we'll take a look at the almost heretical notion of completing this rite of passage at an alternate time.

## Some Herring, Some Schnapps, and You're All Set

Ask anyone (Jewish or not) to describe a typical bar or bat mitzvah and you're likely to get the same basic response:

- The ceremony takes place in a synagogue.
- Many guests, including close and distant relatives, friends, and class-mates, are invited.
- The child sings and chants some or most of the service. He or she is likely very nervous and might sing too fast or too softly.
- Everyone is really dressed up.
- There are speeches during the service, usually delivered by the rabbi and by the parents.
- Etiquette demands that each guest who attends bring a gift for the kid (often a check—extra credit if they mention multiples of eighteen dollars).
- When the service is over, everyone eventually proceeds to some kind of party.

Notice how these answers are just as likely to be given by a non-Jewish person, demonstrating how well steeped the bar mitzvah ceremony is in general pop culture. Furthermore, these descriptions are accurate irrespective of geographical location. Yes, the parties might be fancier in an urban or metropolitan area, and certainly the specific responsibilities of each student will differ based on the synagogue and its affiliation. But painted with broad strokes, these are the basics for the vast majority of b'nei mitzvah ceremonies that take place.

### As an Aside . . .

How do you refer to bar or bat mitzvah in the plural? Actually it's not "bar/bat mitzvahs," although people do say that colloquially. If you know a little Hebrew, you might think that "bar/bat mitzvot" is correct. In fact, because of the rules of Hebrew grammar, the proper terms are:

For two or more boys: *b'nei mitzvah.*

For two or more girls: *b'not mitzvah.*

And perhaps surprisingly, for two or more individuals including at least one boy and one girl: also *b'nei mitzvah.* This is why I use the term b'nei mitzvah whenever possible throughout the book, but will also alternate interchangeably between bar, bat, and b'nei mitzvah.

It wasn't always like this. The way most people envision a bar or bat mitzvah service is most likely a reflection of the modern North American Jewish experience, exemplifying a typical Jewish community's increasing comfort, affluence, and integration within general society.

Generations ago, things were a lot simpler.

Picture a typical Jewish household where the father would attend Shabbat services every week with his young sons. Remember that the female members of the household would not necessarily be expected to go, or if they did, would certainly not take part in the religious rituals to the same degree. Each Shabbat there was a chance that the father might be called to the Torah to receive an aliyah. Because this was an honor reserved for adult Jews (and in that time, adult males), the young son would sit in his place and wait for his father to return.

One week something special took place. The parents realized that their young son had just turned thirteen according to the Jewish calendar, and that meant that he could now be regarded as an adult for the purposes of Jewish ritual. If chosen, now he could receive an aliyah.

On any given Shabbat there are seven people called to the Torah for aliyot, followed by another special aliyah called *maftir.* (More on that very important aliyah later.)

Actually, why leave this to chance? This was an important occasion. During services on this particular week, the father let everyone know of his son's turning thirteen, and he was called up to the Torah for his very first aliyah. It's also likely that the ones who were leading the service (whether a rabbi or other laypeople) made an even bigger deal about this seminal Jewish occasion by calling up the boy in a special way, referring to him as *ha-bachur*

**As an Aside . . .**

An aliyah is one of the most significant honors that a layperson may be given during a service. While other parts of the service may be led by professionals or others specifically trained—like talented laypeople or, of course, b'nei mitzvah students—aliyot are often given to the members of the congregation or other guests in attendance. Literally meaning "going up," it signifies that the congregant is attaining an increased level of holiness (or actually ascending the bimah) as he or she approaches the Torah.

Once there, the individual chants a blessing before the reading of the Torah and then again after that particular reading is concluded. People who are honored with an aliyah are expected to know how to chant the blessings, but there is almost always a large, often laminated version of the blessings, both in Hebrew and transliteration, to lend assistance.

ha-bar mitzvah, the bar mitzvah boy. This way everyone sitting in the congregation would know that something significant was taking place.

In other words, because the boy was now bar mitzvah, that fact was joyously commemorated in public by having him get his first aliyah.

Notice what I just said, and what I didn't say:

- I used the term "bar mitzvah" as an adjective. It wasn't a thing that happened, but rather a description of the boy. You could substitute it with the term "of age" and it would read the same way.
- He did not *become* bar mitzvah when he got the aliyah.
- He was already bar mitzvah before he set foot into the synagogue.

**As an Aside . . .**

There may actually be more than seven people called to the Torah for an aliyah on any Shabbat. Seven is the minimum. While most synagogues do adhere to the rule of seven, it is possible to call any number of additional aliyot in order to honor even more people. Any additional aliyah would be referred to as a *hosafah* (additional). Because there's technically no limit to how many *hosafot* one could add to the Torah service, it's a slippery slope a lot of congregations don't want to put themselves on. The service would last forever.

- The public commemoration was in honor of his changed status, not *because* of the actual aliyah that he received.

Let's delve a little deeper. *Why* was this a cause for any celebration at all? The answer is that this was a true coming-of-age event. In a traditional Jewish community, fathers and sons would attend services regularly, but younger children would have only limited expectations to learn and participate. They certainly picked up a lot by listening to what was going on around them, but with the exception of a few isolated songs or honors traditionally reserved for children, they didn't do too much.

But now everything was going to be different. Because Junior had reached the magic age of thirteen, he could now be a full and equal participant in being counted in a minyan, leading some of the service if invited, reading Torah, and getting called up for any honor.

When this ritual was completed, a number of things might have happened. Everyone present might have congratulated the newly minted adult by spontaneously breaking into song or exclaiming "Mazel tov!" There was a custom, which is still often observed today, of (lightly) throwing candy at the bar mitzvah boy, to symbolize that his life from this day forward should be showered in sweetness. Finally, the father might have made the following blessing at some point during services that morning:

Baruch she-p'ta-ra-ni mei-o-nesh ha-la-zeh.
Blessed be He who has released me from being punishable for this [boy].

That is certainly a strange thing for a parent to recite upon his son's passing a milestone. There are numerous blessings within the liturgy that acknowledge and celebrate our reaching a certain occasion (the most common of which would be the *Shehecheyanu*), but this one sentence seems to be filled with cynicism and legalese. It's possibly a window into the true origin of the importance of setting an age of maturity, similar to why we use either age eighteen or twenty-one in the secular world. There had to be a cutoff at which a person would suffer real and adult consequences for their actions. And by extension, this was the point at which parents would no longer have to be held accountable for their children's actions. Not exactly bar mitzvah card material over at Hallmark.

But in any case, after the services had concluded, all present would make their way out of the room and into some kind of social hall or other general-purpose room in order to recite *kiddush* over the wine and the *motzi* over the challah. Invariably there would be schnapps and probably some other common Jewish foods like pickled herring, bagels, and so forth. (Jewish nostalgia is a multisensory experience.) I'm sure our new Jewish adult was invited to celebrate his new status with shouts of *L'chayim* by all present.

It's important to note that this entire model of how a boy became bar mitzvah and ultimately marked that occasion was something that was reached organically. No one created anything artificial or conjured up some new ritual just for that occasion, and everyone was already in the same place they would have been during any other week.

- The boy didn't need to attend months of lessons to learn how to receive an aliyah.
- The family (or at least the father and son) were attending services anyway.
- The expectation was that they would certainly be there in subsequent weeks but were now able to participate in an even more active role.
- This was a joyful moment for the entire congregation to celebrate, which they did together, in the synagogue.

## So What's Changed?

There have been so many shifts within Jewish life that it's hard to imagine that we even still celebrate any kind of bar or bat mitzvah ceremony. The traditional model that I just described is simply not relevant in any way among countless modern Jews.

Even among the many Jewish families who in fact do choose to affiliate with their local synagogues, a large percentage does not attend services regularly. Consequently there is no longer an assumed basic level of knowledge regarding the service and rituals. And because the week-in and week-out rhythm of synagogue attendance is no longer the routine, there is not any particular distinction between a child's status one week versus their changed status the next. There's no recognition that nothing happened *to* the child; rather, because he or she was now bar or bat mitzvah (read: "of age") this particular week and could be treated differently from that moment on.

Because we've lost so much of the underlying context, the focus has now landed on this *one day* on which we choose to commemorate the crossing of this chronological threshold. And even that day is somewhat arbitrary— often not directly related to the student's thirteenth birthday, but rather chosen on the calendar out of convenience to either the family's preference or, even more likely, the synagogue's scheduling needs. Whereas the marking of an individual's thirteenth birthday was but one stop along a continuous journey, it has now become the destination itself.

There's now an increased and disproportionate emphasis on each aspect of how a child traditionally marked this occasion.

- Instead of this milestone being observed and celebrated with the regular worshippers and immediate family in attendance, families now invite huge numbers of people from all areas of their lives—social friends, professional associates, neighbors, classmates, employers, and employees —without regard to religion or connection to the community.
- Instead of focusing on the fact that a child is now receiving an aliyah because they are old enough, there is a major obsession with the aliyah itself, as if the very act of receiving it has conferred upon the child a new, improved status of adulthood.
- Instead of recognizing that this marks a change in the Jewish community—that there is one more person who is able to be counted among the adults in all ways—people now concentrate solely on the child, as if they have done something utterly remarkable simply by virtue of turning thirteen. The service, the guest list, the numerous speeches, and, of course, the party all exist in homage to this one preadolescent individual. Until next week, that is, when the next student in line will become the object of this larger-than-life level of adulation.

This is all to say that the order of events has shifted to such an extreme degree that we now observe the exact reverse of their original intent. Our main goal with this book is to examine how to get back on track and how to reconcile what used to be a meaningful and significant rite of passage in the path from childhood to maturity with the reality of modern Jewish life. Just because a typical family may not be as active in a congregation (if affiliated at all) or knowledgeable in religious rituals and prayers doesn't mean that there's not a relevant and appropriate way to mark this specific time in a young person's life.

As we go forward, let's ask ourselves some key questions:

- If a family does not regularly attend services and has little connection to members of a congregation, why do we deem it necessary for them to take on the persona of active, observant, and participating worshippers for one particular service?
- Why do we believe that this one service will serve as a launching point for all future participation?

- Why do we place such disproportionate emphasis on the rote memorization of certain prayers and the chanting of specific melodies?
- What typically happens with b'nei mitzvah students and their families in the weeks, months, and then years *after* this one occasion?

We know that all kids have specific interests and talents. In school some opt for choir while others excel on the soccer field. There's student government, drama club, newspaper and yearbook, marching band, and countless other options available for students. In synagogue, however, we typically provide *one path*. Learn and memorize the prayers and a haftarah. Prepare and deliver some kind of *D'var Torah*, a commentary or explanation of that week's Torah portion (most often with great assistance from the rabbi).

Can you imagine if middle schools made band mandatory for every student regardless of whether they ever played an instrument, read music, or even had an interest? We are in effect handing every Jewish kid a saxophone, drilling a number of specific fingerings into their heads, and telling them to blow at a certain time and set their fingers in a certain way whenever we tell them. And then we're surprised and disappointed after the concert is over when they have no real interest in or knowledge of any music or even how to play the saxophone.

In past generations the focus of a bar mitzvah was on a continuation of an existing base of religious knowledge. Because that background does not consistently exist anymore, we must shift our energy into effective and engaging educational strategies. That doesn't simply mean teaching about a bunch of prayers that are likely never to be recited again. Rather, we have to begin the process of creating *a whole Jewish person*—one who will begin his or her first tentative steps in *all* areas of Jewish life: history, community, *tikkun olam* (acts of charity, kindness, and social action), music, Holocaust studies, literature, and, yes, religion and texts. Our kids will not emerge from their b'nei mitzvah experience as experts in Judaism—that's not the point. But by treating them as nascent adults, it's reasonable to expect that they will now be responsible for some level of basic knowledge while still respecting their own talents, interests, and abilities.

# CHAPTER TWO

~

# The Skills

Whenever we have our introductory meeting for future bar and bat parents at our synagogue, I like to joke that during the months ahead they shouldn't be surprised when they hear my voice coming out of their kids' bedrooms. (Newly hired cantors: don't make this joke.) In fact, after more than thirty years of teaching students, I know that my voice has been heard in countless countries and on every single continent. How do I have the time to get around so much?

The answer lies in the way—the same way in each generation—that we have been preparing our kids for their b'nei mitzvah: recordings. There are probably some brave, renegade cantors and tutors out there who have refused to make recordings for their students. Unfortunately, no one has ever heard from these individuals again.

Because the expectation is for the bar or bat mitzvah student to flawlessly chant foreign texts with an unfamiliar melody, it makes it almost impossible for the average child to meet this challenge without a degree of rote memorization. Of course, like any other skill, becoming proficient in chanting the cantillation (commonly known as *trope*) and singing the prayers takes time, dedication, and lots of practice. This assumes that kids are willing to drop or greatly reduce all of their other activities and interests for the months or even years before one important day. If you consider that a lot of students can't even read Hebrew, the task becomes almost impossible without simply memorizing most of it.

And since a typical child's bar or bat mitzvah lesson will last thirty, forty-five, or maybe even sixty minutes a session once a week, it's now understandable why virtually all cantors, rabbis, and other tutors have to rely on their students listening to (and memorizing) recordings of the material. Furthermore, parents expect it.

What should properly be considered a rite of passage—a celebration of crossing a vital and significant threshold—has now become little more than an elaborate play. That week's star takes his place among the other actors on stage, recites lines, and performs actions out of a memorized script. But precious little emphasis is given to one of the most common questions a professional actor would ask: What's my motivation?

I've painted a pretty dreary picture here. So let me hasten to add that it's not always like this. Many families and kids are active and knowledgeable members of their congregations. They are conversant in the liturgy and flow of the service, and in fact, a lot of kids might look at the person leading the service or reading from the Torah and think, "I can't wait till *I'm* old enough to do that!"

These individuals are out there, but I believe that they are the exception among the vast majority of Jewish families. They are the ones for whom the current model of b'nei mitzvah preparation is working effectively and appropriately. As you continue to make your way through this book, remember that my overriding intention is *not* to tear down everything, or to change the entire process just so we can say that we've embraced modernity. Rather, we should look to create more options and a greater variety of *how* and maybe even *when* a child marks this passage.

Before we can really do any of that, we have to take a detailed look at what the typical bar or bat mitzvah student is learning. We throw around the terms *trope* and *haftarah*, but often with mistaken assumptions of what they really mean. In some cases we'll find that today's requirements are nothing more than anachronistic and arbitrary choices that have become mired in the amber of American Jewry.

## The Haftarah

If we were to play a little game of word association, I bet if I said "bar mitzvah" to most American Jews, they would respond with "haftarah." The haftarah is the most iconic, entrenched, and recognized symbol of "getting bar mitzvahed." Still, many people aren't precisely sure what it is, what the text is, where it comes from, or why we're spending most of our lesson time learning it to the exclusion of all else. So before deciding the value of whether or not to chant a haftarah, let's figure out exactly what we're talking about. I'll go into much greater detail on this subject in the next chapter, but for now, here is some basic information.

A lot of the public's misperception is actually a quirk of the Hebrew language, and it could even be confusing to someone who is fluent in Hebrew. The word "haftarah" and the much more familiar word "Torah" have absolutely nothing to do with each other. Each comes from separate roots in the Hebrew language that just happen to sound alike. So, no, the haftorah is not "half the Torah."

In fact, before we continue, we need to figure out how to pronounce the word itself. Most people say *haf-TOR-ah*, which adds to the confusion because it actually includes the syllables and sound of "Torah." However, the correct Hebrew pronunciation of that word would be *haf-ta-RAH*. Both the vowels and accents changed, providing a much clearer distinction from the other unrelated word. This is the reason why I consistently utilize that spelling of the word throughout this book.

How is it, though, that these two words, so related in concept and proximity in the service, are in reality completely *unrelated*?

It all comes down to roots. Every word in Hebrew can be traced down to a three-letter root. (In some rare instances, a root can be two or four letters.) Just as learning Latin helps a person figure out the definitions of so many words in a multitude of languages, so too do Hebrew roots add to a person's comprehension. Even if you don't quite recognize the specific word, if you can discern which three-letter root is being utilized, you can probably take an educated guess.

The word *Torah* uses this root

י ר ה

Y R H

which means "to teach or guide." You can also find this root in the familiar words *moreh* and *morah*, meaning "teacher."

However, the root for haftarah is completely different. It is this:

פ ט ר

P(F) T R

meaning "complete or end." This is because the haftarah forms the completion of the Torah service.

We can then recognize another word familiar to b'nei mitzvah families: *maftir*. You can now see that the words *haftarah* and *maftir* share the same root, and both mean "ending." They're just two different ways of saying basically the same thing—they signify events in the service that come at the end of the Torah reading.

## The Weekly Lineup

As I explained in chapter 1, the weekly Torah portion is divided into seven set readings. For each of these readings, a person (or sometimes a couple or small group, depending on the synagogue and its customs) would be called up and honored with an aliyah. When all seven are read, that week's parsha is considered complete and no more text from the Torah is read.

As they say in so many commercials, "But wait, there's more."

An additional person is called up for an aliyah. Who is this person? Why? Are there seven aliyot or eight?

There are still only seven. This next aliyah doesn't get its own number but instead gets a special name: *maftir*. We know the word means "ending," and sure enough, this marks the ending of the Torah reading. And because it's not a "real" or numbered aliyah, we don't read any new text from the Torah. Rather, we go back a few verses and reread the final part of the last reading. Finally, the person honored with the *maftir* aliyah sticks around and chants the *haftarah*.

That's perfectly clear, right? Is it any wonder why most of the Jewish public and so many of our congregants are confused about what these words refer to or who's doing what and why?

Which of these various and overlapping parts and honors of the service— aliyah, maftir, haftarah—are most connected with the b'nei mitzvah service or would be considered most essential?

## A Minor Detail

Back to basics for a moment. Think back to our scenario in chapter 1 where the boy marks his new status of being of age in the Jewish community by receiving a specific honor in the service that is reserved only for adults: being called up to the Torah for an aliyah. Remember that the act of being called up does not itself imbue any changed status on him; he was already eligible, and his aliyah was a public recognition of the fact.

Since there are seven regular aliyot read each week, he could have been called up for any of them. So how did the bar or bat mitzvah kid get stuck with maftir over all of these generations?

### As an Aside . . .

Depending on the synagogue, there may be rules in place for who can receive a certain aliyah.

Traditionally, the first aliyah would be reserved for a Kohen and the second one for a Levi. Furthermore, because the third aliyah then becomes the first one available for the "general Jewish public," that aliyah itself takes on a higher honor; a synagogue might want to honor a special guest or scholar with this third aliyah. There is also a tradition—not as widely practiced—that prevents siblings or parents and children from receiving consecutive aliyot. As you can imagine, that would be a particularly hard tradition to follow during a bar mitzvah service, where every person receiving an aliyah is likely related.

Remember that I said that the maftir aliyah is not a "real" aliyah. It exists only as a means for someone to be invited to chant the haftarah. However, it would be considered disrespectful to invite someone up to the bimah with the Torah still out and not read from it. So we call this person up, recite the blessings over the Torah, and read something out of the scroll. In keeping with the meaning of the word maftir, the reading from the Torah is now complete.

Because this additional sort-of-but-not-really-an-aliyah does not have the same status as the official seven that came before, we have a little more leeway on who can be called up. According to Jewish law, one could even call up a minor (and in some circles, even a *woman!*) for maftir.

This became a way for traditional synagogues to hedge their bets as to whether a young kid was actually eligible to receive an aliyah. It may seem obvious to be able to figure out how old a child is, but there can be complicating and confusing factors. Their age needed to be calculated according to the Jewish calendar, which had to involve a knowledge of the Jewish months and dates. If the thirteenth birthday fell right on that Saturday, then maybe you had to know what time of day the birth was. Was the child really fully thirteen years old while the service was going on? Some sources in fact say that the status of bar or bat mitzvah only begins on the day *after* they turn thirteen, most likely for that very reason.

So all of a sudden it's not crystal clear whether our newly minted bar or bat mitzvah kid is actually eligible to receive an aliyah or not. The solution to this dilemma was the maftir aliyah. Because of its lesser status, it could be assigned to a person who was still technically a minor. Consider it the just-in-case scenario. And thus the custom was started. From that moment on, every bar or bat mitzvah student would be expected to receive the maftir aliyah and therefore to chant the haftarah that went along with it.

## The Trope

Virtually every Jewish adult remembers hours spent in lessons learning, drilling, and repeating the melodies associated with trope. Let's take a closer look at what trope actually is and how we use it.

Trope, or cantillation, dictates the way that a person chants a certain biblical text. There are numerous trope symbols, which appear under or over each word of the text. These trope symbols serve multiple purposes. First, and probably most important, they serve as punctuation for the text, helping to phrase and parse each sentence so that they make sense. Many of the trope symbols function like commas and, just like in English, make sentences decipherable and comprehensible to any reader.

Next, trope symbols function as accents. Each symbol is not placed randomly under or over the word but, rather, is placed adjacent to the specific part of the word that is accented. This becomes important because the actual meaning of a Hebrew word can vary depending on which syllable is accented. The tropes assure that the correct meaning is preserved. If a person could read Hebrew perfectly but didn't understand a single word, he or she could still sound like a linguistic expert simply by reading the text and adhering to the phrasing and accents of the trope symbols.

While these two functions of trope might not be as widely known, most people are aware that each trope symbol carries a specific little melody. When you see a certain trope on the word, you simply sing that specific melody, and so forth for each successive word. In theory, it could not be simpler. In reality, though, ask any b'nei mitzvah kid (or adult learner for that matter) how many hours he or she spent studying or preparing.

It would be a lot like me telling someone who has never seen a piece of music to sit down at the piano. Here, I say, pointing to some sheet music. This note means you press *this* key. This next note corresponds to *that* key. After I cover all the notes on the staff, I now expect you to play this song for me. Never mind that you don't read music and have never played piano before in your life.

The plot thickens. While many congregants know about tropes and probably even remember a few of the specific trope names from their own past tortured lessons, they may not be aware that there is an entirely different set of melodies for chanting the haftarah versus the Torah. They utilize the same principle but they are not the same skill. And we routinely assume that our young teenagers, their lives filled with a full plate of activities, are going to become fully proficient in what is essentially a new language, within six to nine months of once-a-week lessons.

### As an Aside . . .

In fact, there are no fewer than *six* distinct sets of melodies for chanting the trope symbols. In addition to the more familiar haftarah and Torah melodies, one uses a different melody to chant the Book of Esther on Purim, three lesser-known scrolls on the Three Festivals, the Book of Lamentations (Eichah) on Tisha B'av, and reading from the Torah during Rosh Hashanah and Yom Kippur. To make it even more fun, there are various times when the reader needs to switch from one set to another—sometimes *mid-sentence*.

Students spend a *lot* of time in b'nei mitzvah lessons learning and drilling trope and how to sing the various melodies. And parents expect (or at least hope) that when their kids are finished with the process, they'll be knowledgeable in the subject and able to sing any haftarah or Torah reading. The reality is that this is rarely the case. And what's even more surprising is that the parents themselves experienced this identical training process—remember, this model of b'nei mitzvah training is largely unchanged going back multiple generations—but somehow hope their own children will come out with a different result.

The ideal is that students learn and become proficient with the system of tropes. The general premise is that we teach the kids how to sing each trope symbol. They not only apply those melodies to their own haftarah but are then able to learn *any* haftarah. After all, only the words are different; the trope melodies are easily identifiable and remain the same in each text. So, yes, if you really become proficient with the tropes, then you should be able to apply them to and sing any haftarah that comes up during the year.

Why isn't it that simple?

Often, parents have this expectation that the b'nei mitzvah students won't just memorize their haftarah, but that they'll really learn the tropes (seemingly forgetting that they themselves never did that during their own b'nei mitzvah lessons years ago). Synagogue professionals often highlight this aspect of training as well. But at the same time, they insist and expect that recordings of everything be provided "to help practice." Of course, most kids—especially the efficient and most organized ones—listen and sing with the recordings and end up memorizing the haftarah.

Well-meaning parents are just one side of this. The b'nei mitzvah teachers and tutors take part as well. Simply put, it's the path of least resistance. It's so easy to provide the recording, have the student make regular progress through the haftarah week after week, and perform wonderfully on the day of the bar or bat mitzvah. Literally everyone is happy. The parents are thrilled (and relieved) their kid got through it. A smooth and well-chanted haftarah makes the synagogue's clergy look good, and they can point to yet another success story. And the congregation can boast about the quality of their students.

So what's the problem? Why would anyone want to take an entire room full of happy and satisfied Jews and rock the boat? The answer: because no one is really sure what the student learned and how any of it can be used or applied after the service. In the next chapter, we'll take an even more detailed look at the haftarah and why it's the thing the student is least likely to ever look at again.

## Teaching to the Test

What I'm describing is nothing new. We see it constantly throughout a child's education and exposure to standardized testing.

Look for instance at the infamous SAT test. Teenagers and families know that the score that a student receives—whether fair or not—is one vital indicator of which colleges they can get into. Predictably, they will pursue any avenue that will maximize those scores. (Fortunately, actually cheating or buying your way up is pretty rare and limited to crazy news stories.)

An entire industry has arisen to address this need. Parents pay big bucks to educational centers or tutors to prepare their kids to ace the test (which also exacerbates the chasm of opportunity between those that have the means to do this and those who don't and are therefore at a handicap). Note that the focus is only peripherally and superficially on learning the material. The true goal is to learn *how* to take the test. This involves learning to master the insider strategies on eliminating multiple-choice answers, knowing which questions to skip and come back to, and understanding how the test is scored so that it may be more beneficial to skip a question rather than to guess.

Now compare that with how we've become accustomed to preparing our kids for b'nei mitzvah. While we pay lip service to the idea that we want our kids to master trope, in reality we're teaching them how to memorize it more efficiently. We tutors use multiple strategies—marking certain trope symbols with colored highlighters, utilizing trope and Torah software, underlining accents, transliterating words for those students whose Hebrew reading isn't quite as proficient—to bring our kids to the level that all parents and congregants expect. It's not so much educating taking place as getting a student to *appear educated*. The bar or bat mitzvah ceremony is the test, and we are teaching exclusively to that one occasion.

## The Services

Jewish kids begin learning how to lead parts of the service from their very first days in Religious School. But just as in all the other skills we've already talked about, most (and really, usually all) of this education revolves around rote memorization: learning to chant a text, often from a recording, and being able to parrot back the correct words with its tune. If a student or layperson is able to achieve that, then we say that they're leading the service.

Part of this phenomenon is the tension that exists between having professionals in charge of the service (that is, the cantor and rabbi) with wanting to create an accessibility for everyone to take part. So we begin teaching the prayers to little children, we have Religious School classes take over Shabbat services, we assign Sisterhoods and Men's Clubs certain weekends where they're in charge of leading the entire service, and, of course, we prepare b'nei mitzvah students to show that they're now Jewish adults by having them take on the responsibility to lead some or all of the service on the day of their celebration.

It seems like a logical choice. Indeed, we cantors spend a great deal of our time teaching this material to congregants of all ages. But before we ask, "Should all of our b'nei mitzvah students lead the service?" I think a better question to start with would be this:

*What does it actually mean to lead the service?*

Consider this a Jewish educational existential question. Is a person who is "leading" the service really leading it at all?

Take two individuals: one is a professional cantor and the other a congregant who doesn't understand a word of Hebrew but whose reading is flawless and singing voice is pleasant. On the surface, both could stand on the bimah while chanting the texts to the proper melodies, and it would be a meaningful and enjoyable experience for everyone present. What's the difference between the two? Does it matter?

At first glance, it's a positive experience for everyone. The congregant has the honor of leading the congregation in worship. Those in attendance are happy to have one of their own act as sh'liach tzibur—the person who leads the service, literally "representative of the public." The proper melodies and musical modes are used, and the words are pronounced without any mistakes. The cantor is happy because she gets a chance to sit back and pray like a "regular person" for a change while someone else takes her place at the podium. Furthermore, she looks great to all present because one of the measures of a synagogue's success is the degree of lay participation. This is an A+ scenario for everyone.

So does it matter that the otherwise capable congregant who is leading the service actually has no idea what any of the words mean? Additionally, he is not knowledgeable about the history of the specific prayers that he's chanting, why they come in the siddur at that time, or why he's chanting a particular melody.

### Raising the Bar

Take just one prayer—it can be a single paragraph or excerpt—and really figure out what it means. Ask yourself a set of challenging questions:
   Is this the way modern Jews think?
   Why is this in the service?
   Can you rewrite the prayer using only your own words?

And so it is with our b'nei mitzvah students and their preparation for the service. Even for the small percentage of kids for whom the current model works very well and fits in with their interests and aptitude, we're still teaching them not how to really lead a service but, rather, how to be a talented parrot. They are taught to look like they're leading a service.

We have created a *Potemkin service.*

You might respond by pointing out that this is simply a particular synagogue's or school's failing; that of course students should be taught not only how to read a word, but what that word means. Or to put it another way, a bar or bat mitzvah child can lead the *Barchu* prayer while also knowing that it is the public call to worship that begins the main part of the service. There's opportunity to teach not only the *how* but also the *what* and *why*.

---

### As an Aside . . .

A Potemkin village refers to a location where the buildings' facades are attractive and well maintained, but in fact there's nothing real behind them. Things appear a certain way, but there's nothing of substance within.

---

And you would be right. Even using the existing model of b'nei mitzvah preparation, we could do both: teach a child how to sing a prayer while providing the meaning and context of that text. But that takes time. And the current expectation is all about the quantity of "bimah time," and less, if not in fact nothing at all, about the depth and quality of knowledge. The paradoxical truth is that the more I could effectively teach a student to lead (that is, *really lead*) a service, the less he or she would actually do. The existing model of b'nei mitzvah preparation is a zero-sum game. Every minute teaching one subject is one fewer minute spent doing something else.

Going even further, leading a service while having no real knowledge of what anything means runs counter to any interpretation of Jewish tradition or how the modern worship service came into being. Our Jewish sages anticipated the idea of laypeople attending services with the right intention to pray, but lacking the necessary skills. And they provided an elegant solution, which can be summed up in a single ubiquitous word: "Amen."

Centuries ago, siddurim—prayer books—were not a commonly accessible item. Even the ability to read wasn't universal. The texts of the prayers were known only to specially trained scholars who could recite these little-known texts. Yet Jewish law mandated (and still mandates) that every person was responsible to worship three times a day. How could an average Jew fulfill this requirement if they not only didn't have the resources to possess an expensive volume of the liturgy, but wouldn't be able to read it even if they did?

The *halacha*—Jewish law—provided a way. One person—the model of the modern cantor—would be knowledgeable and capable of reciting all of the texts properly, and all those in attendance would listen and respond "Amen"—a way of saying, "Yes, I agree." In this way, with one single word, Jewish law considered it as if they themselves had recited the prayer and therefore had fulfilled their requirement. The word "Amen" was the legal equivalent of saying each word. But that entire paradigm is built upon the assumption that the person actually saying the words knew what they meant and had the appropriate intention. It would be religiously pointless for those in attendance to say "I agree" to something that the leader recited but had no idea of its meaning. Unfortunately, that's precisely what takes place in virtually every b'nei mitzvah service.

Seen in this light, a bar or bat mitzvah service isn't really a service at all—but it looks and feels like one. It's a Potemkin service. The student looks like they are leading, sounds like they are leading, and the congregation responds as if they are leading, but no one has any knowledge or understanding of the words. Can or should a person say "I agree" to a text when no one—the congregant or the person saying the words—has any idea what the words mean?

One of the goals of this book is to identify ways that we can take aspects of a process that has become increasingly distant and irrelevant and transform them into something meaningful and understandable. This is the way that connections are formed and pave the way for an adult relationship with our rituals and traditions.

# CHAPTER THREE

~

# The Haftarah

It is amazing how much time and effort we make our kids spend on a skill that in most cases is completely useless. I would estimate that more than 75 percent of most b'nei mitzvah students' time in lessons is devoted to drilling and memorizing a text to which they have no connection, and will not have much use for throughout the rest of their lives.

## What Is the Haftarah?

As I explained in the previous chapter, the word "haftarah" has no grammatical connection to the word Torah. Instead, it means "completion" or "ending," in that it takes place at the end of the Torah service and serves to close out the readings from the Bible.

Another source of confusion for both kids and adults is what exactly any given haftarah is about. The weekly Torah reading is much easier to follow. Its characters are often familiar and the events take place chronologically. That is, we leave off one week with a given set of events or story and pick everything right back up again the following week. We read the Torah in order throughout the year.

But the haftarot (plural for haftarah) don't adhere to any narrative arc from one week to the next. Sometimes a story might be familiar to some congregants while others are completely unknown. And who are these names that we come across: Ezekiel? Hosea? Habakkuk?

Some of the answers lie in the layout of the entire Bible, which is known in Hebrew as the *Tanakh*. The word Tanakh is an acronym comprised of the Hebrew letters:

תנ ך

Corresponding to the English letters:

**T N Kh**

Each letter stands for a distinct section of the entire Bible:

**T**orah
**N**evi'im (Prophets)
**K**etuvim (Writings)

Obviously the first section—Torah—is the most familiar and probably contains most of the characters, episodes, and narratives that the average Jew could name. Ironically, it's also the shortest section, comprised of only five books—the so-called Five Books of Moses.

In contrast, each week's haftarah is not taken from the Torah at all. Rather, it comes from a book found in the Nevi'im section, which is why it's sometimes called the Prophetic reading. It features texts dealing with a given prophet or other period in Jewish biblical history.

### As an Aside . . .

The third section of the Tanakh—Ketuvim (The Writings)—is not read on a regular basis during services. Nevertheless, many of the books of this section are indeed familiar to many congregants. The Book of Esther, which is read on Purim; all of the Psalms; Proverbs; and other important books are contained within Ketuvim. Many of the prayers that are recited during services are taken from or based on excerpts from Ketuvim.

## Why Include the Haftarah?

The basis for our weekly Torah reading is well established. It has its origins in the book of Nehemiah (found in the Ketuvim—Writings), which laid out in a step-by-step manner the way in which the Torah would be read to the assembled public. Indeed, a close reading of those verses found in the eighth chapter of Nehemiah bear a close resemblance to our own modern service where we take the Torah out from the ark, raise it up in front of the congregation, and read a portion of the text so that everyone present can hear it.

In fact, reading the Torah and giving the people access to its teachings became such a priority that it was instituted not only during Shabbat, but also during the week on the busy market days of Monday and Thursday. None of this included any of the books from Nevi'im.

There were probably a couple of reasons why the later books of the Prophets merged onto the Torah reading as part of a weekly ritual. First, all of the emphasis so far had been on the five books of Torah, with little to no time spent on this much larger second section of the Tanakh. Therefore, a certain excerpt from one of the Prophetic books was linked to every single Torah portion, ensuring that congregants would be exposed to that material as well.

It wasn't just random. The early rabbis connected the haftarah thematically to that week's Torah portion. That might mean that the Torah and haftarah readings dealt with the same idea—such as kingship, military victory, or the mention of a certain character, for instance—or just took place during the same time of the year.

### Raising the Bar

Sometimes the connection between the week's Torah portion and the haftarah is obvious, while other times the reason why that particular text was chosen is more subtle or esoteric. A great exercise for b'nei mitzvah students (and for the lay worshipper as well) is to read the Torah portion and the haftarah all the way through in English and see if they can figure out the relationship between the two texts. It would be even better if the student came up with a logical answer that was actually not the original reason why the rabbis chose it.

Going back through the various periods of Jewish history, there was also another practical reason why the haftarah was read. During times of persecution, the study of Torah might have been forbidden by hostile rulers, who were aware that Jews would include such reading and study during their weekly Sabbath services. As a way of getting around this prohibition, it was possible to read other texts, like from the Prophets, in place of the actual

Torah reading. This preserved the Jewish people's devotion to biblical text while still adhering to the decree of the authorities.

All of this certainly paints a logical and compelling rationale for why we include a haftarah in each week's service. What's less certain today is why we insist on teaching this to our b'nei mitzvah students, often to the exclusion of all other material.

We already know *how* this started—in chapter 2, I explained that the maftir aliyah was a good choice for someone who was likely but maybe not definitely old enough to receive that honor. The question is *why* has it persisted when we can know perfectly well exactly how old a child is. We don't need to reserve this lesser status aliyah any longer.

## The Varying Lengths

A major criticism of the way we structure the preparation for b'nei mitzvah students is that the entire process is completely uniform—a one-size-fits-all endeavor that doesn't take any individual's level of ability or interest into account. How ironic, then, that the major piece of that preparation, the haftarah, can vary wildly in length.

While the rabbis were fairly consistent in assigning a haftarah to a given Torah portion, they were all over the place in determining how long each Prophetic reading would be. Some haftarot are barely one page long, while others go on endlessly for four or five pages.

Imagine this: take every bar or bat mitzvah student in a synagogue's class in a given year and line them all up randomly. Within that line, you'll have boys and girls whose interests and skills vary wildly. Some will have learning issues, while others might suffer from anxiety at the thought of standing in front of a large group. Some might read Hebrew fairly well, while others might recognize only a few letters. Some might come from active temple families who attend services regularly, while others have no connection to or familiarity with the service.

Still, each one of those thirteen-year-old kids is an individual with unique needs and talents who deserves a relevant and meaningful way to form a relationship with Judaism. And they all have a bar or bat mitzvah coming up in the near future.

Now, let's go down the line, figure out when each kid's birthday is, and based on that information assign them a logical Shabbat on the calendar that matches up the closest to the date at which they turn thirteen.

Everyone have their date? Good. Now, let's look at the Jewish calendar— in Hebrew, called the *luach*—and find out which Torah portion is read on each child's date. Since every Torah portion has a corresponding haftarah, we can then continue down the line of kids and hand every student the haftarah that belongs to their week.

Some kids will get a single sheet of paper. Most will get two or three pages. A couple of doomed students will be handed pages and pages of Hebrew text.

There's no consideration of whether a child might be dyslexic, not read Hebrew fluently, or in fact loves a challenge and would think "the longer the better." Furthermore, it might take one of these kids just a month or so to learn a short haftarah, while someone else will spend every moment trying to complete a lengthy portion, and even then not be able to master the entire thing. Sorry—it was bad luck and a quirk of the Jewish calendar.

In fact, this wasn't some theoretical exercise. *This is exactly the way that most b'nei mitzvah kids have to deal with learning a haftarah.*

You might suggest a solution, some kind of workaround. Especially in synagogues with smaller classes and more flexibility, why not purposely choose a date that better reflects each kid's skill? One family could proactively choose a week with a long haftarah for their child who is more capable. Others could aim for those weeks with a less-challenging haftarah.

But in fact, all that this accomplishes is to allow some families to game the system. It does nothing at all to improve or enhance the experience or education. Instead, it just eases the already familiar path for some kids. And realistically, who gets to decide who ends up with the shorter, easier haftarot? Is it a free-for-all, first-dibs kind of thing? More problematically, does the rabbi or cantor decide which kids are likely to be capable to learn more and who should be steered toward the lighter load?

## Some Solutions

You might already be thinking of an easy fix to the issue of wildly varying lengths of the haftarot. Why not abbreviate them? It's true that there is a set haftarah that is associated with each Torah portion. But there are both traditional and nontraditional options available to make them shorter and more accessible to students of varying abilities and interests.

Many synagogues already routinely utilize a triennial cycle for Torah readings, whereby a third of each portion is read throughout the year. Then the following year the next third of each portion is read. Over the course of three years, the entire Torah will have been read publicly in services, after which the cycle repeats. This is what I would describe as a quality-of-life issue in services. It makes it much easier for the people (b'nei mitzvah kids, adult shul goers, or synagogue professionals) who must master a reading each week.

Similarly, services can be a lot shorter, and congregants don't have to sit through interminable readings some weeks. And it provides more flexibility in assigning readings to kids and adults.

We could also institute a triennial cycle for the haftarah as well, which is actually done in some isolated congregations. As in the case of the Torah reading, this would make chanting a haftarah more accessible and seek to level the playing ground from one week to the next.

Next, we have what I like to call the "Sephardic escape clause." There are often slight or substantial differences in the text of the haftarah based on whether one follows the Ashkenazic tradition (probably as do most of the people reading this book) or the Sephardic tradition. In many cases, the haftarah is the same, but partway through the text there is a notation that "the Sephardim end here." So, that is already a pre-sanctioned and logical place to end, especially if the Ashkenazic version goes on for a lot longer.

Finally, a more out-of-the-box idea: Why not chant or recite the haftarah in English? Later in this book we'll look at various changes—both minor and major—that we can make in order to reimagine the way that b'nei mitzvah kids can connect with the material. One obvious idea is to expose them to Biblical text and the message of the Prophets in a language that they actually understand. Going even further, most English translations are horribly awkward and in many cases need translations themselves. Instead, a student could recite the whole haftarah—in English and entirely in his own words.

## One and Done

Even if we could somehow get around this troubling method of assigning haftarot to kids without any consideration of ability, the whole process still doesn't make much sense.

Let's go back to asking ourselves what our goals are, like I suggested in the introduction.

*If* we are still intent on requiring every child to chant the haftarah, what is the intended goal? What are we trying to accomplish with this task?

Assuming that one of the most compelling objectives of b'nei mitzvah preparation is to learn a new skill in order to take part in services in a more involved way, the haftarah is probably the very worst choice and absolutely least useful thing to learn.

Why?

Remember that each haftarah is unique to that particular Torah portion. So a child's haftarah—even if she learns it flawlessly—will only be recited once a year on that one Torah portion. There will rarely be any opportunity for the student to come back to services and chant it again in a future year. And even in an ideal situation where the temple's calendar is free and the student is available, capable, and willing to chant her haftarah again, it could only take place on one Shabbat a year. That's the *best* we can aim for.

It's true that most cantors and b'nei mitzvah tutors do try to teach the process of learning and applying the trope melody to all haftarot. So theoretically, one goal of b'nei mitzvah preparation would be the ability to chant not just one haftarah, but *any* haftarah.

That sounds great in theory. But as we've figured out already, that's just not the way most kids work. Parents will insist on a recording, and students will learn, memorize, and drill their own haftarah. The current model emphasizes the end goal of the performance, not the process of learning and absorbing the method.

And even for that small percentage of individuals who are interested and musical, and who would be able to sit down with a haftarah from any week and learn it, this skill is still the least useful. There are just not that many opportunities throughout the year to chant a haftarah. If the synagogue has a big class, there will be other b'nei mitzvah scheduled on most weeks. In other locations, there are other congregants who might volunteer to be called up for maftir on a specific week. An active, dedicated, and especially talented teen might be lucky to be assigned to do a haftarah once in a great while. But the vast majority of kids—think of the thousands upon thousands of our Jewish youth who celebrate b'nei mitzvah every year—will simply *never* look at a haftarah again.

## A Modest Proposal

One doesn't need to tear down all of the existing models of b'nei mitzvah training or even completely reimagine what we teach our kids (although we'll certainly do a lot of that later on). All synagogues, kids, parents, and tutors could take this one modest step and dramatically improve students' religious education without addressing any other problem for the time being. This is the low-hanging fruit of effecting a change.

Here it is: *Stop teaching the haftarah altogether.*

Simple. Easy. We can even imagine the collective sigh of relief that is washing over every thirteen-year-old Jewish child in North America.

Instead, concentrate on the Torah reading. For every reason why learning a haftarah is a useless skill, the ability to read Torah presents numerous opportunities and potential utility throughout one's Jewish life.

While the haftarah is a set length (often really long), Torah portions are usually much shorter. In fact, the maftir reading (as explained in chapter 2) is almost always merely three or four sentences long. Yes, there are exceptions throughout the Jewish calendar, such as various holidays and special Shabbat weekends when a separate maftir reading with a specific theme is chanted. Because these readings can be quite lengthy, the bar or bat mitzvah student in these cases could simply be assigned any other non-maftir reading. That's a perfect length with which to introduce a beginning student to the concept of trope, and have the luxury of being able to take one's time with practicing a brand-new skill without the pressure of multiple additional pages looming over the horizon.

For some students, that one short reading will be plenty. For others who are able to master the reading, there are more readings available. The beauty and utter logic of replacing the haftarah with Torah reading as the main focus of training is that it utilizes the same basic skill (mastering cantillation) with the flexibility of matching the amount of material to the interest and ability of the child.

Additionally, this first modest step also allows for greater participation and involvement *after* the b'nei mitzvah. Whereas there was little to no realistic chance that a student would ever chant a haftarah again, Torah readings are much easier to assign to former students. It's true that the actual reading would be different than the one originally learned, but that's the whole point. With the emphasis on learning one short reading very well, each kid will better master the process and be able to apply that to other new and short readings. It piles success onto success and provides a path for those students who would like to be continually involved in religious life.

Notice that this is simply one modest change in strategy. It doesn't address the bigger issues discussed throughout this book. Replacing the emphasis on the haftarah with the much more logical Torah reading still tells us nothing about each student's personality, interest, background, or likely future life as a Jewish adult. If we go back to our example of handing every kid a saxophone and saying, "Here, play this," then all we're doing is varying the length and content of the music that we're shoving in front of them. Then we're hoping that as a result of that change, they'd be more likely to pick up the sax again in the future because their experience was slightly more positive.

## Looking Forward

The last few chapters have been described as "Where We've Been." By definition then, this has been a look backward. In order to make any substantive changes, one has to appreciate how we got here and have an understanding of the context where this framework exists. Picture this first section of the book the same way you would view those fading pictures that are glued into your grandparents' photo album. Just as we can chuckle at the questionable fashions of the time, those garish outfits, and ubiquitous cigarettes, so too should we begin to think of most current models of b'nei mitzvah training.

Our next section will concentrate on the present. While the fashions are more current, and you won't see any cigarettes in the pictures, we will be able to identify a lot of the factors and dynamics that exist in modern Jewish life.

PART II

~

# WHERE WE ARE

# CHAPTER FOUR

~

# The Synagogue

The modern American synagogue is the de facto center of Jewish life in most communities. The primary litmus test of a family's involvement and dedication to Judaism is whether or not they have joined the local temple. There's a certain feeling of pressure to support the Jewish community by affiliating with a synagogue, regardless of one's personal religious observance or knowledge of the traditions. In fact, this is an extension of the one-size-fits-all model of b'nei mitzvah training. All of the guidance comes from the top down: We know what's best for you. We know what's best for the Jewish community. Your personal interests and abilities are not as important.

This is a strange chapter for me to write. I have been a full-time cantor and synagogue professional for my entire career. My livelihood is based on the current model. If new families did *not* routinely feel the need to join a synagogue, what would happen to me? Am I writing myself out of a job? The answer is no—the path forward is not to stop leading but rather to lead and teach in a different way. I refuse to take the position that any Jewish professional will be threatened with unemployment because a new generation of Jewish adults has found a way to become more educated and connected with their religion and culture.

And in any case, I'm more concerned with the next generation of Jewish leaders, professionals, and individuals. There are hints out there that Jews are increasingly dissatisfied with the status quo of synagogue life. They view the denominational lines that divide us as artificial and tribalistic. They perceive a certain hypocrisy in being told to unquestioningly adhere to a set of religious regulations when in most cases this is simply not practical or compelling in modern American life. And they recognize that the vast majority of synagogues and congregations place these expectations on the clergy—the rabbi and cantor. One humorous but all-too-real example is the congregant who is eating in a restaurant and sees her rabbi at the next table and complains to the temple board that the rabbi was eating out in a treif (nonkosher) restaurant. No one thinks to ask the woman why *she* was eating there in the first place. The cynical assumption in many temples is that the congregation is paying the clergy to be religious for them.

And most significantly, because of all the reasons put forth in the last section, most Jews are woefully, painfully undereducated and ill prepared to function as modern, learning, and evolving Jewish adults. Much of the adult Jewish population is, in fact, frozen in time as thirteen-year-old Jews. They are still mired in the quicksand of their largely irrelevant and now-useless b'nei mitzvah training. As a result, when their own children reach that age, they naturally expect them to receive the very same training that they did.

## What Denomination Are You?

Oh, the volumes that could be written on this one seemingly innocuous question. In a lot of ways, this could be the most divisive and destructive issue that faces our current Jewish population. Many Jews are more comfortable identifying by what they're *not*, rather than where they truly fit.

If you ask the average Jew-on-the-street to define the three most familiar denominations or movements in Judaism, you will likely receive some version of this response:

Orthodox: very religious

Conservative: sort of average, most of the service is in Hebrew

Reform: not religious, mostly in English

I don't mean to exclude my friends who belong to a Reconstructionist synagogue, and who emphasize that being Jewish, in addition to its obvious religious aspect, also involves identifying with a distinct people and culture. But these "big three" categories are the ones that would be most identifiable to most Jews.

Furthermore, members who affiliate within these denominations are quick to point out the differences that exist between them and their fellow Jews. Growing up in a Conservative congregation as a kid, I distinctly remember hearing about "the church on the hill." Was this a reference to a greater awareness of our interfaith neighbors? Not a chance. It was the term used for the nearby Reform synagogue that had a long, sloping, uphill driveway. I suppose it's human nature for a group to bolster their own sense of belonging by expressing ways in which they feel superior, but such words are offensive and only serve to further divide us.

A cynic once defined a Conservative synagogue as a congregation full of Reform Jews led by an Orthodox rabbi. There's actually a lot of truth in that statement.

One reason why the current process of training b'nei mitzvah kids is outdated and increasingly irrelevant is that most Jewish adults themselves are adhering to an outdated model of Jewish affiliation. If you engaged in a discussion about why a certain Jewish family chose to affiliate with a given movement, you would undoubtedly hear the word "authentic" mentioned numerous times. Other responses would likely include phrases like "that's how I grew up" and "more comfortable and familiar with the service."

In other words, we're training our kids a certain way for exactly the same reasons we join temples:

- It's expected.
- We think it's authentic, and no one is saying otherwise.

- It's the way we did it when we grew up.
- We derive satisfaction from the quantity of material our kids learn because it sets them apart and makes them superior to other kids.

The reality is—and if there's one controversial line in this whole book, here it is: A large number of Conservative Jews are in fact Reform Jews. When asked to identify or characterize their Jewish observance, theology, spirituality, involvement, or priorities, I believe that a significant number of self-identifying Conservative Jews would answer in a way completely consistent with Reform Judaism.

And just as we can't even accurately figure out who we are and where we fit, we're passing along the same ambiguity and uncertainty to the next generation. We know we're *supposed* to do and feel a certain thing in temple, so we're also *supposed* to teach you a bunch of stuff.

## It's the Law

The Hebrew word *halacha* refers to the code and body of Jewish law. For instance, one would say that according to *halacha*, it is forbidden to drive on Shabbat or eat pork.

The subject of *halacha* helps to identify where each denominational movement stands. Stated broadly, the Conservative Movement defines itself as dedicated and committed to *halacha*—which means that a true and committed Conservative Jew would never take a bite of nonkosher food and would observe all of the restrictions and laws of Shabbat. Certainly, how that law is interpreted, and possibly changed, marks a key difference between the Conservative Movement and more traditional or Orthodox branches.

Reform Judaism states (again, broadly) that each community possesses the authority to define its connection with tradition and ritual, in keeping with the needs and customs of modern society.

Which definition would resonate most with modern American Jews? In fact, a chief difference between the Orthodox and Conservative movements is not the level of observance or how the services take place—they would be mostly the same or at least very similar. Instead, what sets these two groups apart is more esoteric and theological. Did God dictate or write the words of the Torah, or did man? Were they divinely authored or divinely inspired? Is *halacha* absolute and unchanging, or is there a process by which to amend Jewish law while still respecting its authority over Jewish life?

# The Road to B'nei Mitzvah

How do we assess whether a certain synagogue is successful or thriving? We look at their Religious School. When we observe a temple that has a large Hebrew School enrollment and many b'nei mitzvah kids each year, then we say that the shul "is doing well." Conversely, we turn a pitying eye on those temples mostly populated by older people, as if there's simply no future there and their days are numbered. Among Jews, there are often two questions that they'll eventually ask each other: (1) How many members does your temple have? (2) How many kids are in your Religious School?

## As an Aside . . .

Is the proper term Hebrew School or Religious School? I suppose the two terms are interchangeable, but Hebrew School may sound a little old-fashioned. I personally don't have a preference between the two. I think substituting the word "Religious" implies that the education is more general and not solely about learning Hebrew skills, but in reality the model is pretty much the same regardless of its name.

The success of a synagogue is perceived to be directly connected to the size of its student population. As a result, in many cases synagogues have been transformed into b'nei mitzvah assembly lines. Everything else exists to serve that most vital of functions. Young families are invited to attend. They are recruited for membership by offering a reduction in dues or even eliminating them altogether for the first year or two. Often, young kids can initially be enrolled in the Religious School without having to be members. Later, when the kids have progressed through certain grades, membership is required.

In the meantime, the all-important b'nei mitzvah dates are handed out to families a certain period of time in advance—usually a few years. The Hebrew School curriculum lends itself to pre–b'nei mitzvah training, in that kids are taught how to read Hebrew and how to lead parts of the service. B'nei mitzvah lessons, then, become a seemingly logical next step in Jewish education.

Every step along the way is intended to lead a family into the Hebrew School and culminate with that most Jewish graduation ceremony: the bar or bat mitzvah. No matter how often a rabbi delivers the cliché "this is not the end, but rather just a beginning," everyone present in the congregation knows the same thing. This is usually the end.

The synagogue itself strongly delivers that message. Regular Religious School attendance usually continues through seventh grade and then stops. There are no more b'nei mitzvah lessons. Engagement with families who have "aged out" drops off precipitously. Of course, this is not an ironclad rule. Some temples do have high-school educational programs and youth groups with robust involvement. But these are considered discretionary and extra-curricular activities. Attending Hebrew School during the week, though, is expected and assumed.

## Mandatory Attendance

It's impossible to deny the connection between regular service attendance and a certain level of comfort at b'nei mitzvah services. Of course, it's only logical. When kids and families attend services often, they obviously hear the same prayers over and over, they learn the melodies (even just passively by listening), and even more valuable, they know what happens at a service—where people stand, what comes next, who does what, and so forth. Compare that with a family who makes the (equally valid) choice not to come to services much at all, and then walks into the sanctuary on the morning of the bar or bat mitzvah. It's a bit of a deer-in-the-headlights situation. They're not even sure where to sit, let alone how the service will proceed.

So if your goal is scoring a top-notch performance at the bar or bat mitzvah service, then, yes, it is absolutely in your interest to come to services as often as possible.

Many synagogues have taken this sensible idea and actually made it a requirement. Administered either through the Religious School or the b'nei mitzvah training program, all students are obligated to attend services (Saturday morning or Friday evening) a set number of times during the year leading up to the ceremony. I cannot express how much I disagree with this policy.

I am a professional, full-time cantor who works in a synagogue. *Of course* I want everyone to attend every service. Families, teens, little kids, senior citizens—nothing makes me happier and adds to my own prayer experience than a sanctuary filled with congregants. Furthermore, we do everything we can to encourage increased attendance. We plan class services. We vary the melodies. We invite (not require) special groups to participate. We schedule speakers. We try to provide multiple reasons for people to attend.

But as soon as we make services just another obligation—another piece of homework—then we've gone off message. We are in effect telling people that services are such a chore and so unenjoyable that you would never want to come on your own. Therefore, we're requiring your attendance. It's for your own good. You'll thank us later.

And it's a meaningless obligation anyway. All temple families know that there's no way to enforce such a requirement. There has never been nor will there ever be a bar or bat mitzvah family that's told, "Sorry, we need to reschedule the ceremony. You didn't attend services the proper number of times over the last year." So some well-meaning families will make the effort because they're good rule followers, while others will get away with less. And that takes away from the entire policy for everyone.

And again, the underlying message is that attending services is the most important way to demonstrate one's Judaism. We don't require our kids to join a temple committee or perform meaningful acts of social justice (the often-required community service project is usually a token activity that's superficially tackled during the months leading up to the b'nei mitzvah). Instead, we're implying that you're coming up short by not attending services on a regular basis.

How do you monitor attendance anyway? In a congregation that adheres to traditional Shabbat observance, it is forbidden to write anything on Friday night or Saturday morning. This produces a bit of a challenge to record an individual's attendance. So synagogues where it's forbidden to write have had to come up with increasingly convoluted methods of keeping track. The most popular are:

- One designated person (rabbi, cantor, teacher, or someone else who drew the short straw that week) has to keep a school roster and little pack of stickers in their pocket. After each service, they can put a little sticker next to the name of every student who is there.
- There is a box filled with index cards with each kid's name on them. Each service, a child finds their card, removes it from that box, and places it in *another* box that will be looked at later. This proves they were there that day.

Then you get into all the fun. Parents contact the office during the week and say that they went to another temple for a relative's bar or bat mitzvah—can they still get credit? A cadre of parents or teachers is assigned to guard the box of index cards because some kids are taking their friends' cards and putting them in the second box even though they weren't there (they will eventually grow up and punch their coworkers' timecards at work). Some parents figure out that they've been making the concerted effort to attend all of the different services multiple times while other families that they know practically never do—and no one seems to care or give any kind of consequence.

Can you see how ridiculous this all becomes? What started as a sensible and admirable idea of encouraging families to attend services has devolved into a meaningless and laughable attempt at enforcing yet another vapid task and obligation. And with each increased step of record keeping— (1) write all the names on index cards; (2) keep all the cards in a box; (3) have every kid find their card and move it to another box; (4) make sure each kid is only taking their own card; (5) supervise the cards; (6) during the week, make note of each card and then return them all to the original box— we are moving further and further away from any family's intrinsic desire to *simply attend services because they might actually be meaningful and enjoyable.*

The title of this chapter is "The Synagogue," and like much of this book, it makes an assumption about the parents and children who are preparing to become b'nei mitzvah. We are presuming that they have chosen to affiliate with a synagogue and must then conform to the rules and norms of that community. But this leaves out the very significant population of the Jewish community that *doesn't belong to a temple at all.*

As you can imagine, this dramatically changes the dynamic. A family can schedule a bar or bat mitzvah ceremony at their own convenience, unfettered by the limitations of a temple calendar. They have wide latitude in choosing who will tutor their child, what material will be covered, and the format and location of the service. It's another example of what many call "à la carte Judaism," where the "consumer" has the power to choose all aspects of the business model instead of relying on how things must be done or how they have always been done.

This introduces an enormous opportunity for creating an alternative experience, but it provides a number of drawbacks as well.

## A Community Affair

I've always felt that above all else, a young person (at whatever age) who becomes bar or bat mitzvah is now able to take their place among the established members of the Jewish community. But how does one define the word "community"?

The more familiar approach, as described earlier, is for a family to affiliate with a synagogue and become members of a congregation. Ideally, the family

## Raising the Bar

When a synagogue requires families to attend services, the implicit message is that they would rarely attend otherwise. And why is that? Because in many cases, the services are indecipherable to those who are not proficient in the tradition or language. Furthermore, services are often too long—it's a tough sell to convince an average family to give up three hours on a beautiful Saturday morning to sit in a dark sanctuary and be sung at and spoken to.

While not the primary focus of this book, we can come up with numerous ways to make services more appealing to the average Jewish family without sacrificing tradition or Jewish ritual.

Out of many possible suggestions, I propose what I think would have the most impact: make the service shorter. Is this a strange thing for a professional cantor to say? There are so many ways to accomplish this.

Feel free to abbreviate certain portions of the service. These could even function on a rotating basis so that over the course of several services, all the texts would be recited.

If a synagogue has not done so already, adopt the accepted triennial cycle of Torah readings, whereby a third of every portion is read each year.

Does the service include a sermon, or more informal D'var Torah? I do think teaching has an important place, but perhaps that could be accomplished in less time or outside of the actual service. Some congregations have a study session over lunch immediately following services.

Most controversial: abbreviate the haftarah. We've gotten into this elsewhere in the book, but there are a few ways to go about this, and some actually have a historical basis.

Is there an optimal duration for a Shabbat morning service? I honestly think no longer than ninety minutes would be perfect and is something that could be accomplished by instituting certain changes. Alternatively, a temple could designate one Shabbat a month as the "express" service. See what kind of attendance you get then.

will become involved with the temple as well as other members of the congregation, both socially and religiously. At the same time, the children will enroll in the synagogue's Religious School and will progress through each grade, culminating with the b'nei mitzvah year—when the entire class will celebrate their b'nei mitzvah throughout the year. That's our conventional model—and all other issues aside, it indeed provides a sense of community. The families celebrate with each other and with the rest of the congregation.

But we can expand our definition of what community means. Outside of synagogue affiliation, an individual can simply identify as a member of the Jewish people—one doesn't need a temple or Religious School for that. Therefore, a more private gathering comprised of a family's circle of relatives and friends would also be an appropriate way to mark a young person's entering into an increased role within the Jewish religion.

However, the same potential drawbacks exist as in the more conventional synagogue model. Whether preparing with their temple's cantor, or with an independent tutor who is hired just for the occasion, the student is still likely going to be memorizing a set of material by rote with little additional knowledge.

Families might choose not to join a synagogue for a variety of reasons. They may deem the steep cost of membership to be an insurmountable barrier, one which does not reach the top priorities of the household. They could assume that they would never attend that much anyway—maybe on the High Holidays—so what would be the point? Or they might consider themselves nonreligious, secular, or simply ethnically identifying Jews, for whom a temple membership just will not be something they are interested in.

So it's ironic that even among this last group of nonreligious Jews who do choose to pursue a bar or bat mitzvah for their children, most of the time they still seek to emulate what would take place in a synagogue. Here is a group that, by definition, exists outside of the cookie-cutter Jewish educational experience, and most still assume that it's simply required for all thirteen-year-old boys and girls to learn some prayers and a haftarah or Torah reading and chant everything at a service. The pull of generational tradition is strong on everyone, irrespective of synagogue affiliation or connection with Jewish observance or ritual.

Consequently, non-synagogue Jewish families engage a b'nei mitzvah tutor, schedule lessons, arrange for a venue (perhaps a hotel function room), invite their circle of friends and family, and stage their own service officiated by clergy whom they've hired for the occasion (cynically referred to within Jewish professional circles as a "rent-a-rabbi"). The outcome is the same: they can say their child was "bar mitzvahed" or "bat mitzvahed," but there was very little change or growth accomplished, and the result is a superficial experience. It's ironic that even nonreligious families have been taught to feel that a bar or bat mitzvah ceremony must be religious in nature.

And then there are examples that draw on a combination of these factors. Sometimes a family that belongs to a synagogue will still opt (if allowed) for a more private service. For instance, they may choose to schedule a nonstandard time for the bar or bat mitzvah, perhaps during a Saturday afternoon or evening when there would be no regular service taking place. In this case, they are in effect renting out their synagogue's sanctuary in order to have a ceremony that would be attended only by their invited guests and likely no other members of the congregational community.

Yes, there may be valid educational and personal reasons for doing so. Some kids have an increased sensitivity to noise, commotion, and the usual stimuli that would take place at a busy and crowded Saturday-morning service. Closing in the circle and quieting down the environment would be an effective way to address those issues.

Other times, the intention—although well meaning—still misses the point. Because parents are under the impression that all b'nei mitzvah must be identical and must include a prescribed set of skills, then, for whatever reason, they may decide that their child will not be able to master all of that material (or will struggle and do a "bad job"). In that case, they might preemptively decide to opt for a more private venue within the synagogue so the child can focus on a smaller number of pages and Hebrew texts. There's a vague and unfortunate feeling of underlying shame in these situations, as if the mere thought of meeting their children where they are and aiming to master a smaller number of pages is something that must be hidden from the rest of the congregation. And without a doubt, the bar or bat mitzvah kid is well aware of this dynamic and internalizes the fact that their achievement carries a metaphorical asterisk forever afterward.

Because so many of these decisions are based on what's going on at home, we need to take a closer look at what may be going on within each family.

# CHAPTER FIVE

~

# The Family

Jewish professionals are tempted to look back fondly on some kind of golden era of Judaism—a vague Catskills-esque atmosphere when everyone dressed up for services, the sanctuaries were all decorated with dark wood, and the rabbi was a revered older man with a beard (and his wife, the rebbetzin, would be active in the Sisterhood).

What else was typical? Everyone belonged to a temple. When a young Jewish family would move into town, they would automatically seek out and affiliate with the local synagogue. It would be unthinkable for them not to do so. Whereas the last chapter focused on the synagogue, here we can look more closely at the kinds of families that either choose to affiliate with a synagogue or, because of a variety of circumstances, are unable or unwilling to do so.

## The DIY Movement

So what's changed? We still have synagogues of course, and many Jewish families choose to join. When their kids are young, the parents begin the assembly-line process that culminates in the bar or bat mitzvah ceremony— just as it's always been.

But not everyone.

Increasingly, twenty-something young adults who have just moved out and begun their professional careers, living with a partner or newly married, don't feel any compelling need to seek out a synagogue. Perhaps they still feel a connection to their family's temple where their parents may belong. More likely, they can't imagine or simply aren't able to pay the substantial cost of belonging to a temple. Nostalgia is wonderful, but if that's all these young adults feel, it's certainly not worth a couple thousand dollars a year. It doesn't matter that no synagogue would ever turn away a young family for financial reasons. (Indeed, many synagogues extend free membership to newly married couples.) It's difficult to have to make arrangements for reduced dues each year. It's a lot simpler not to join in the first place.

Even those young couples who could easily afford the cost ask themselves some basic questions: Why join? What value will we receive? Often, they conclude that synagogue membership is just not worth it. It's a lot like health insurance and cell phone plans: many young adults find it much easier and more practical to stay connected with their parents' affiliation than to initiate their own connection from scratch. Why join a synagogue and pay dues (including the dreaded and ubiquitous building fund) when you get to attend with your parents? Their family rabbi and cantor would also likely be available for weddings or baby-naming ceremonies.

And this isn't to necessarily say that Jewish life is dying. Far from it. Everything that I've seen shows me that younger Jews are craving a meaningful connection to tradition and ritual. What's changed is how they go about accomplishing that connection. Because they are products of the b'nei mitzvah assembly line, this shouldn't come as much surprise.

We've devoted all of our time and effort into having these kids memorize and drill prayers and trope symbols. We've spent precious little time (or no time at all in many cases) actually finding out what each individual is interested in and where they might find a long, lasting connection to a life of Judaism.

Let's create a hypothetical scenario. I'll go out of my way to make it seem like a best-case outcome—what would be considered a significant success in Jewish life. Even so, it will show how our current synagogue and b'nei mitzvah model of education is ultimately coming up short.

## Sarah's Story

Our imaginary protagonist, Sarah, grew up in a Conservative Jewish household. Her parents kept kosher at home (but ate anything out). Of course, they belonged to the local synagogue. In fact, because living a Jewish life was so important to the family, her parents settled in a town with a strong Jewish presence. They even had a choice of which synagogue to join, as there were a number of various temples that affiliated with different movements.

Having grown up in a Conservative synagogue themselves, they predictably made the same choice.

Sarah excelled in Hebrew School. She loved the songs, she quickly mastered Hebrew reading, and she would often be the go-to kid when her class was asked for volunteers to lead services. Her family attended services regularly as well, so she was a constant presence in the building.

Each summer Sarah had the opportunity to go to a Jewish sleepaway camp, so she had a vast number of Jewish friends from all around the region in addition to those in her community.

She also eagerly anticipated her bat mitzvah. Lessons with the cantor were a breeze, and she quickly had the haftarah and Torah reading down. Her speech, written with the help of her rabbi and information she and her parents found online, detailed some personal connection to the Torah portion. Sarah also performed a community service project that was required by the temple. With the bat mitzvah service now completed so successfully, Sarah's parents enrolled her in the temple's high-school program and youth group.

When it came time for college, Sarah purposely chose one that had a significant Jewish student population and an active Hillel on campus. While there, she became involved with other Jewish students and attended services at Hillel. Oh, and of course she only dated Jewish guys.

So let's pause for a moment. Is there anyone reading this who doesn't feel that this is a perfect, ideal situation? I purposely infused this imaginary person and her family with almost every positive facet of Jewish life:

- Regular synagogue attendance
- Religiously observant household
- Excelling at (and enjoying!) Hebrew School and bat mitzvah lessons
- Jewish sleepaway camp
- Post–bat mitzvah education and involvement
- Youth group
- Active in Hillel in college

I think I threw everything possible in there—I certainly could have had Sarah attend Jewish Day School as well, but I wanted to make this vignette resonate with the largest possible amount of people.

Let's continue. So where does Sarah stand now? She finished college, landed her first job, and moved in with her (Jewish) boyfriend. Both of them are clearly on the marriage track, but that will wait a little bit until they are more settled in their careers. In the meantime, they are living in or near a major city, somewhat close to the suburban towns where they grew up.

By any measure, this is a dream come true for most Jewish families (especially the Jewish boyfriend part). What in the world could anyone find wrong with this? Is there anything negative going on?

I don't mean to pick on Sarah or her parents. They did absolutely everything perfectly and accomplished all that was expected of them. Sarah undoubtedly feels a connection to Judaism, and she likely still keeps in touch with a lot of her old camp friends on Facebook, or whichever social media platform her demographic uses at the time. She doesn't remember much about her bat mitzvah, though, and certainly wouldn't be able to chant a haftarah or read Torah without a great deal of assistance, including a recording. But the whole process was extremely positive, and just thinking about her bat mitzvah and how well she did brings a smile to her face.

But let's dig a little deeper. While Sarah had a positive Jewish experience and upbringing, there didn't seem to be much creativity. No innovation. No new ground covered. There were certain things that were expected of her and her parents, and they completely met all of those challenges admirably.

What's next for Sarah? And therein lies the problem. She was brought up to be a part of Jewish life that does not necessarily resonate as much with a large number of Jews. All we've really prepared Sarah to do is repeat the exact same pattern. Move to the suburbs, join a temple, and send her future kids to Hebrew School. Sarah has lived a Jewish life of *what* and *how* but has received no education in *why*. She has mastered the mechanics of being Jewish. But is this all that we want our kids to get out of Judaism?

If Sarah follows the pattern that is common among her peers, she will soon start to question why it's necessary for her to join a temple. What does it mean to be Conservative when she and her friends certainly don't observe any sort of Shabbat rules? Why do Jews insist on labeling people in the first place? And yes, when it comes time to get married, she'll either ask her parents' rabbi or cantor to officiate or simply find one to hire for the occasion. And in the true spirit of DIY religion, Sarah might just ask a close friend to officiate—it's incredibly simple to go online and become a member of the clergy in five minutes.

Sarah's experience with Judaism is almost exclusively skill based, and all of those skills were taught, drilled, and performed as part of her bat mitzvah preparation—during her lessons and Hebrew School years. Now that she doesn't require those skills anymore (there's not a lot of demand to read Torah at her IT job), her connection to Judaism is bereft of any substance. While it may be a positive experience, it's mostly nostalgia.

We have prepared Sarah to read, recite, and chant. Not to question. Not to tap into her skills and interests and *passion* and find new ways to express her Judaism. The bottom line is that much of what Sarah has been taught is nothing more than how to join a temple and attend services and repeat the identical pattern with her future spouse and children.

And of course, what about Sarah's Jewish friends? Most of them did not follow that same path. Many of them simply endured their Jewish childhood and did whatever they were told to get through their b'nei mitzvah. At that point they were relieved to have the burden of Hebrew School lifted. A bunch of her friends ended up in a relationship with non-Jewish partners, so even if they wanted to become involved with a synagogue (even one that actively welcomes all families), it's still an added hurdle and an unspoken (and, too often, a spoken) stigma to endure.

Once you remove the previously unquestioned step of synagogue membership from the occasion, things begin to unravel quickly. With a minimal connection to anything Jewish that exists outside of the synagogue and b'nei mitzvah preparation, Judaism becomes a situational experience, usually surrounding life-cycle events.

The logical conclusion is that the bar or bat mitzvah itself can be viewed as just another required life-cycle event, not requiring synagogue membership. Hire a tutor for lessons. Book a hotel or other venue for the service. Arrange for an officiant to lead services. And that increasingly common and attractive option: plan a destination bar or bat mitzvah.

## The Family Unit

Unlike our imaginary friend Sarah and her parents, not every family falls into such a simple category. Many children have parents who are divorced, and they must balance a life between two homes, each with its own opinion about or emphasis on religious education and commitment.

The stories are commonplace, and any of us who have been synagogue professionals for even a short time have experienced our large share of these situations. Here are just a few examples of complicated situations that would seriously impact any child's progress or motivation:

- A student regularly shows up for lessons without his materials because they were left at the other parent's house.
- One parent is coordinating (and paying for) every aspect of the bar or bat mitzvah without any support from the other.
- One parent is actively working against the other in having the bar or bat mitzvah at all.

- There is a history of domestic abuse and there is a restraining order forbidding one parent's attendance. Now there needs to be a contingency plan on how and when to involve law enforcement or private security since that parent has threatened to attend the ceremony.
- The parents are divorced and one or both have remarried a non-Jewish spouse. Now there are step- or half-siblings who are not Jewish and need to be involved in this ritual that is completely foreign to them.

One reason why the generations-old model of b'nei mitzvah training is no longer relevant in many cases is that it's primarily based on one traditional model of the family. For children who live in blended families, or who have to navigate more than one household, or whose parents are in financial difficulty—the usual synagogue-based model might be ill-suited for them. In these situations it would be valuable to have different options for how to pursue a path into Jewish adulthood and connection that do not necessarily focus on attendance at services or membership in a synagogue. In chapter 10 we'll go into greater detail on how that might work.

## The Destination Bar Mitzvah

The Destination Bar Mitzvah does sound exciting, I know. And for those families who are in the financial position to consider it, it sounds like an ideal solution to . . . well, pretty much everything. While I would assume that the most common example would be having a ceremony in Israel (in Jerusalem or on Masada), there are many more possible and exotic destinations that parents can choose. It combines the excitement of a family trip with a much reduced guest list and doing away with all the hassle and planning of a traditional service and party (see chapter 8 for all that fun).

This book is all about options. It's about saying b'nei mitzvah do not all have to look a certain way. Anything that meets a child and family where they are, matches with an individual's needs and interests, and helps to form a connection to Judaism and foster one's identification as a full-fledged member of the community is on the table.

One drawback, then, of destination b'nei mitzvah is that it typically removes community from the equation. The way such a trip is usually structured takes a child *out* of his or her community and emphasizes only the ceremony, in a remote location. Furthermore, aside from the change in venue, there's not much innovation—it involves taking our usual and dated model of preparation and service and simply relocating it to another place. The focus is still on drilling, memorizing, and ultimately reciting a bunch of skills that will still likely be discarded soon after the family passes through immigration and returns their passports to the drawer. Adding to that disconnect is the fact that the family usually contracts with some officiant—a stranger who will arrange the tutoring and then lead the service.

I would feel much more positive about such a trip if it ventured off the beaten path creatively as well as geographically. Here are just a few possible ways that destination b'nei mitzvah might be reimagined and reinvented:

- Especially for countries other than Israel, do some research on the Jewish history of the location. Was/is there a substantial Jewish presence?
- Do you have any relatives or ancestors who came from this country? What happened to them? Can you visit a location where you know some family lived?
- Find out how the music or literature of that country might have influenced the way people prayed in services.
- Can you team up with another family to make this journey, thereby adding a measure of community?

I find material like this a lot more compelling than the usual trip to the Kotel (Western Wall) in Jerusalem. It's certainly an incredible and worthwhile destination in itself (God forbid anyone think I'm telling them not to visit Israel), but staging a worship service there seems just as inauthentic as pretending to be religious at home—and perhaps even more so. Depending on the arrangements of a Kotel bar mitzvah, it might take place within the context of an Orthodox worship service. Given that the visiting family is unlikely to identify as Orthodox Jews, this can serve to further disconnect the bar mitzvah boy and his family from a strong Jewish experience. But regardless of the specific arrangements, it's an imperfect solution to the family that may not affiliate with a congregation—and it's still putting the synagogue and the service front and center in the process.

Just as I pointed out in the last chapter, families that would otherwise consider themselves nonreligious and nonobservant are still structuring their children's b'nei mitzvah through a traditional lens. Whether the event takes place at a hotel, at the Kotel, or on the beach in Cancún (which admittedly doesn't sound so tough to take), there's still that feeling that unless you have an officiant, a service, and some memorized lines to recite, it is an inauthentic experience.

# The Modern Family

The heading for this section was intentionally vague. The "modern family" is simply any family living today. We have been spending a lot of time high-lighting the fact that kids are individuals with specific talents and interests. So too is each family a distinct unit. Our reimagining process needs to meet them where they are as well.

As I've pointed out, we'll get into more specifics on possible paths later on in the book, but here I want to emphasize how preparing for b'nei mitzvah need not be a solitary undertaking. We can all picture the typical bat mitzvah kid coming home from lessons ("How was your lesson?" "Good.") and then disappearing into her room to practice (and that's our best-case scenario). Singing, preparing, and memorizing are all considered homework that she must do to get ready for the following week.

So often I have heard parents tell me, "I never hear him practice," or the similar but subtly different, "He never lets me listen to him practice." If this takes place in a family with some non-Jewish members, or with parents who live in separate locations, the sense of isolation is magnified. Rather than seeing it as the obstacle to preparing for b'nei mitzvah, as many people would, this is instead a perfect opportunity to personalize the process and increase its meaning and significance.

I believe strongly that a child does not prepare to become bar or bat mitzvah alone. Rather, this is something that should involve the entire fam-ily—irrespective of marital status, the presence of different religions in the household, or anyone's skepticism or feeling of alienation from religion or belief in God. Think about it; if we are saying that one true objective is for a young person to announce that they are now entering Jewish adulthood, then that must be a family process. Connecting to something on an adult level should mean being able to communicate, make decisions, and articulate one's passions, beliefs, and doubts. This includes entering into conversations with those who have alternate opinions or feelings about Judaism, or who aren't even Jewish at all. This entire piece is lost when a kid goes into their room to practice (memorize) and considers their homework done.

## Raising the Bar

Especially within the Conservative Movement, there seems to be a lot of ambivalence toward non-Jewish members of the family—we accept; we tolerate; we secretly judge. All of these attitudes result in the fact that we often don't know how to properly include them in b'nei mitzvah ceremonies. We welcome with one hand and use the other to keep them at arm's length. More than that, a lot of synagogues have stated policies of exactly when a non-Jewish guest or relative may ascend the bimah, if at all. The underlying message is that this is a worship service devoted to Jewish ritual—therefore it is necessarily reserved for Jewish people and no one else may be considered a full participant.

Instead of this somewhat limited and, in my opinion, chauvinistic sentiment, let's instead throw our b'nei mitzvah doors wide open for all friends and relatives of different faiths. Imagine a situation where Adam, a typical bar mitzvah boy, gets up in front of the congregation and delivers his prepared D'var Torah about his portion and what he learned from it. I guarantee that both Adam and every single member of the congregation (including Adam's family) will forget the substance of what he said within weeks or even days.

Now reimagine. Adam's parents are divorced and his mother remarried a non-Jewish person with kids. This is traditionally a "problem" situation in Jewish life—maintaining a Jewish household with non-Jewish siblings. But if we adopt an attitude of inclusiveness and don't simply send Adam to his room to practice behind a closed door, then we begin to be presented with incredible opportunities. Reimagine Adam's bar mitzvah, but this time the D'var Torah has been cowritten by Adam and his non-Jewish stepbrother who lives in the same house. They stand on the bimah together, and we hear from Adam's brother what Adam taught him about Jewish values and morals and how they successfully navigate their religious paths—how they exist together and how they diverge. That's unforgettable.

# CHAPTER SIX

~

# The Lessons

Can any sentence strike more fear and excitement into a family's life than "It's time to start bar mitzvah lessons"?

No matter what kind of synagogue we're talking about, or even if a family doesn't affiliate at all with a congregation, some kind of bar or bat mitzvah training is part of the process. The time spent in lessons in the months or year leading up to the bar or bat mitzvah ceremony is as much an accepted ritual as the ceremony itself. And just as we've come to expect a uniform experience at the service, so too do the lessons conform to a usual structure. It's interesting to note that an increasing number of families and educators rally against the institution of standardized testing in schools, which includes valuable classroom time devoted solely to preparing for a certain exam— so-called teaching to the test—and yet that is exactly what is taking place during each session the b'nei mitzvah students spend in lessons. When we treat a bar or bat mitzvah as an accomplishment, an objective to be achieved, then the lessons are not truly about education but about *preparation*.

Indeed, this is exactly the language we use.

No one ever asks a thirteen-year-old student, "What are you learning for your bat mitzvah?"

Instead, the usual questions (I find them often posed by well-meaning grandparents) are invariably:

"So, are you ready for your bat mitzvah?"

"Do you know your haftorah yet?"

Or the dubiously helpful "Don't worry; you're going to do a great job." (Thanks a lot, Grandpa. I wasn't really worried until you told me not to worry.)

Even with students for whom the current model of b'nei mitzvah training is suited—that is, kids and families who love singing and learning about prayers and who already are involved in services—b'nei mitzvah lessons are just that: lessons. There is very little educational material presented. Most of the time is spent drilling, listening, repeating, and being told to go home and practice more.

Again, this is not to disparage any cantor, rabbi, tutor, parent, or, least of all, an already busy and stressed-out thirteen-year-old student. Everyone is doing the best they can working under a system that exists to train an individual to perform. (And of course, some kids love to perform! Most others—not so much.)

## How Lessons Are Set Up

Some synagogues are huge institutions with many b'nei mitzvah students, while other, smaller ones or those with an older population may only celebrate a handful. But irrespective of size, all temples will have some system in place to prepare (always that word, not to *educate*) their soon-to-be-thirteen-year-old kids for a bar or bat mitzvah service whose date was probably assigned up to three or four years before.

The specific details will certainly vary depending on the congregation. Some lessons may take place up to a year beforehand while others may last six or nine months. They may be thirty, forty-five, or sixty minutes (and sometimes just fifteen minutes), and students will see the cantor (if that temple employs one), the rabbi, or other tutors who are on staff.

## Don't Make a Mistake!

It amazes me how much time and effort is expended into making sure that a nervous, out-of-place thirteen-year-old kid standing up in front of a large crowd and singing in a foreign language *never makes a single mistake.*

—Pronounce that word again.
—No, you missed that vowel.
—Repeat that tune with me. Again.
—You have to stand like this.
—Slow way down; you're singing too fast.
—You're not loud enough.

## As an Aside . . .

When I attended cantorial school and trained to be a professional cantor, I spent years learning countless nuances of the liturgy and the proper *nusach* (modes and melodies for the prayers). We delved into texts as well as sacred and secular musical history. At that time, very little time was spent on pedagogy or any kind of preparation to teach b'nei mitzvah students.

It's amazing to look back over a decades-long career and realize that a huge percentage of the time I've spent performing my job has been dedicated to teaching kids and preparing them for b'nei mitzvah, versus how much time has actually been spent singing on the bimah. Fortunately, I know that modern cantorial training reflects this more realistic vision of how many clergy spend much of their time.

I am reminded of this story—perhaps apocryphal—of a cantor who served a large and important congregation in the 1950s. A young cantorial student approached him with trepidation and asked, "Cantor, what is the most important thing I can know about teaching kids?" The cantor gave a dismissive look and haughtily responded, "I don't teach children."

That answer wouldn't fly in today's world, where many synagogues (especially the larger ones) have become virtual b'nei mitzvah factories.

I have no idea where this obsession with perfection came from. I have often asked beginning students what they're most excited and most nervous about for their b'nei mitzvah service. Of course, the answer to the latter question is always making a mistake or messing up—and more specifically, making a mistake in front of all their friends who are in attendance. That's a lot of pressure for a middle-school kid to carry.

The vocabulary that we use reinforces this pressure.

No one looks back on a bar or bat mitzvah and says, "Wow, you learned so much."

Instead, relatives, friends, and temple members all say the same thing—and even before you read the words that are coming up, you know what I'm going to say—"You did such a good job!"

Everything that we say and all the words that we use are structured around the fact that a child's bar or bat mitzvah is a one-time performance.

- Kids don't *learn* subjects or material. Instead, they *prepare*.
- Kids don't seek out material of interest to them or do any sort of exploration. Instead, they *attend lessons*.

- Kids don't demonstrate that they grew or developed as a result of this experience. Instead, they did a *good job*.

---

### As an Aside . . .

I always find it amusing—but prudently keep it to myself—when the canned "You did such a good job!" response is used regardless of the circumstance. Some kids just . . . don't. Everyone has experienced at least one cringeworthy bar or bat mitzvah experience (or should I say performance). When the entire process is modeled more like a weekly Broadway show rather than a true demonstration of educational achievement, then it stands to follow that some kids will knock it out of the park while others will want to slink off the stage. Still, every kid gets to hear, "You did such a good job!"

Often, a congregation will have a board member or officer represent the temple leadership and make a presentation to the student during the service. Chosen ahead of time, this individual will have prepared some remarks for the occasion. Sometimes, this presentation will follow an hours-long ordeal of mangled Hebrew and butchered prayers, but even so, every speech opens with "Wow, you did such an amazing job this morning!"

To paraphrase Garrison Keillor's classic line, "Welcome to our synagogue, where all of our b'nei mitzvah kids are above average."

---

It's ironic that kids and parents live in such abject fear of not being 100 percent perfect. Even within the current model of b'nei mitzvah training, and even if we're assuming that much of the process and most of the material is out-of-date or not well suited for the present, there's actually one vital and relevant skill buried within the entire production: that of public speaking.

If we take out the fact that memorizing and then reciting a haftarah by rote might not be the best use of time, there is value in having a student—of whatever age or talent or ability—learn a little about how to stand up in front of an audience and speak. In later chapters, when I get into much more detail about possible ways to reimagine and restructure what our kids learn, I'll spend some more time on public speaking. Currently, it's not treated so much as a discrete skill but more of just something to get through in order to endure the couple hours of bimah time.

When I teach kids during lessons, I utilize what I think is a unique approach. As a kid learns (or usually memorizes) the text and gets to a certain level, I often sit back and just listen to her sing. That means letting my

**As an Aside . . .**

As someone who has vast experience with both public speaking and funerals, I find this quote by comedian Jerry Seinfeld to be completely accurate: "According to most studies, people's number one fear is public speaking. Number two is death. Death is number two. Does that sound right? This means to the average person, if you go to a funeral, you're better off in the casket than doing the eulogy."

student make her way through whatever text we're working on and have the opportunity to butcher a word, get tongue-tied, or otherwise forget how to sing something. At this point she'll look up at me, perhaps waiting for me to issue some mild disapproval (as if I ever do that), or, more likely, hoping that I'll give her the proper pronunciation so she can get through it and continue.

My approach is more holistic. I want to hear what the whole thing sounds like, not just that one phrase. Again, in looking for any kind of important life skills within the questionably limited curriculum that we are forced to teach, I am attempting to have my student look beyond the specific words in front of her, and instead of learning only how to pronounce a Hebrew word, that, more valuably, she *learns how to make a mistake*.

This is a hard concept for kids and parents to wrap their heads around. They are under the impression that every fiber of b'nei mitzvah training is centered around presenting a flawless performance. Can you imagine the pressure that puts on a child? It comes as no surprise that I have had kids literally in tears because they mistakenly turned two pages at the same time and started chanting the wrong paragraph.

Do you remember this scene in the 1987 movie *Wall Street*: Michael Douglas is speaking at a shareholders meeting and announces, "Greed is good. Greed works." I feel exactly the same way about mistakes that kids make during the service. "Mistakes are good. Mistakes work."

While each family is necessarily focused on the one all-encompassing day when all of their friends and family will be present for their child's service, I have the luxury of looking at the bigger picture. What are services like each week? What creates the most positive experience for worship among the congregation?

I've come to a conclusion that sounds counterintuitive: a bar or bat mitzvah student who performs flawlessly and who sings through every word with fluency and complete accuracy is simply not as interesting as one who mangles an occasional word; who needs to look back at me a couple times during the service to be reminded of a tune; who steps off the bimah carrying the Torah and nervously bolts down the aisle instead of slowly processing, causing everyone to smile and chuckle as they all lunge toward the center and try to kiss the Torah before it races by.

Mistakes like that reflect the student's personality and may be the only factor that sets apart each cookie-cutter bar or bat mitzvah service every week.

So I teach the kids not to avoid making any mistakes, but rather *how* to make them:

- If you get stuck on a word, get yourself unstuck.
- If you think you just sang something wrong, just keep going.
- If you start a tune wrong, continue—either get back on the right tune or just keep singing it in whatever way.
- If you lose your place, take a moment to find it. It's not like anyone's going anywhere.
- If you forget what to do, look back at me on the bimah and quietly ask.

These directions sound pretty obvious, but it's amazing how programmed our kids are to view any deviation from perfection as a failure. During lessons that take place closer to the bar or bat mitzvah date, we can start practicing "run-throughs." If you were preparing to deliver an important speech, you would find it helpful to stand at the actual podium and be in the room where that speech was to take place. Similarly, we move out of my office and into the sanctuary, so my student can stand on the bimah at the podium and feel what it's like in that room.

During these sessions, I have to get them out of the habit of stopping every two seconds ("Was that right?") and to simply continue.

## The Parents

One might think that a chapter entitled "The Lessons" would concentrate solely on what takes place in the tutor's office and how we currently prepare kids. Nevertheless, it's necessary to devote an entire section to the parents—the unseen but hugely influential partners in this process. It's amazing to consider the effect one or two people can exert on lessons and b'nei mitzvah expectations and almost never set foot in the office.

Let's break this down.

# In the Room Where It Happens

Should parents attend lessons with their child?

This is actually one of my favorite topics to discuss because, as opposed to a lot of the other areas that I cover in this book, there is no uniform, agreed-upon way to address this subject. While the answer seems incredibly obvious to me, many of my clergy and educator colleagues are split on their preference.

So before I give it away, let me pose the question to you:

You are about to begin lessons with a new student. After setting up a day and time with her mother, she asks you if she should come to the lesson as well. This way she can keep track of her daughter's progress and make sure she's concentrating on the material—while providing the added benefit of the mother picking up a lot of the information along the way just by listening and being present.

What do you think I'm going to say?

My answer (presented politely, of course) is NO, NO, and NO. Thanks for your interest, Mom. Please stay away.

The reasons stated above are usually the ones given by my colleagues for *wanting* to have a parent in the room. It helps to include them in the process and provides more of an opportunity for a family-wide educational experience. Additionally, when a parent is present for lessons, you prevent any misunderstandings about what you expect for the next week. It gets rid of the "I didn't know you wanted me to practice that" moments, and helps absolve the teacher in any "But you never told me to" situations.

## As an Aside . . .

Of course, we must be cognizant of the realities of today's world and acknowledge that there are other valid reasons why a parent might wish to be present in the clergy's or tutor's office during a one-on-one lesson.

All of us in the educational world are well aware of commonsense procedures, including never being alone in the building with a student (important to consider when scheduling evening lessons when the building would otherwise be empty) and always having the office door at least partially open. Some tutors teach out of their homes, which certainly presents a distinct list of challenges. So keeping in mind this important subject, I'm limiting my opinions to the educational and religious benefits of whether or not a parent should be present.

My parent-in-the-room proponents would be perfectly correct if our entire objective was to memorize some text and repeat it back to me, and, ultimately, the congregation. And they, along with all of the b'nei mitzvah parents, could certainly be forgiven for thinking just that. So whatever we have to do to make that happen is how we should proceed. Having a parent present would probably add motivation and discipline to a student's progress, so why not encourage it?

My perspective is a little different. Even if nothing ultimately ever changed in the entire b'nei mitzvah experience, and even if we continue this exact status quo for the next generation (a depressing thought), I would still say that my prime objective in lessons is *not* to have my students master a Hebrew text and learn how to sing it perfectly. That may be the outcome (and is definitely what I would be aiming for), but the true goal is not to teach the student to *do* it, but *how* to do it.

Let's take this to an absurd extreme. Imagine that a bunch of rabbinical scientists (we'll leave the cantors out of this) invented a "b'nei mitzvah pill." A couple weeks or so before their b'nei mitzvah, each kid could take this pill, go to sleep, and wake up the next morning with a perfect grasp of the material. (Some of my students already try this by falling asleep to my recordings and figuring they'll know it when they wake up.) What an amazing invention! Upon waking up, a student can chant the entire haftarah flawlessly and can sing all of the required pages. There'll be no mistakes and no stress, and the effects of the pill will never wear off. Just show up on the morning of the service and sing it all.

If you're a Jewish professional, would you give your student this pill?

If you're a Jewish parent, would you give it to your child?

I believe that many would opt for this path of no resistance. It would certainly make the entire process a breeze. All of the common problems that kids, parents, and tutors meet along the way—not practicing enough, the burden of scheduling and attending lessons, the stress and worry about every little mistake—would all be avoided. Each student would perform marvelously for his or her parents, family, friends, and congregation. And the rabbi and cantor would be thrilled because no one—parent or congregant—would ever have a reason to complain about any kid's lack of preparation.

But of course you see how this is a ridiculous solution, even if such a thing did exist. While everything about the current b'nei mitzvah model process screams "results, results, results," it's the actual process along the way that is most important. I believe that all families *want* their kids to learn, connect, and to find meaning in taking on an increased set of responsibilities—even if we are all collectively stuck in an outdated and often irrelevant way of achieving that goal.

Another reason why I find it counterproductive to have a parent in the room is because a parent can be *too* interested. Even though this same material (trope, haftarah, siddur) has been taught for generations, there are often differences in the way that it is taught. The system of cantillation—trope symbols—is a fascinating subject in itself and goes well beyond a student mindlessly memorizing and reciting the tune for *Mahpach Pashta*.

Parents who are present in the room may remember their own travails in learning these melodies a few decades ago but now find the whole subject interesting and engaging. (This is perhaps a further argument for postponing the age of b'nei mitzvah. So much of this is simply lost on younger people who aren't yet able to appreciate the wonderful nuances of what they're learning.) These parents, then, begin to participate in lessons themselves. They want to engage, ask questions, learn more. What a wonderful opportunity for furthering one's Jewish learning. But not during the time set aside for lessons, unfortunately. I have seen parents proceed to dominate the time with the student, who then predictably and gladly takes a quiet back seat to what's going on around them.

But even if the parent merely sits there and remains quiet, I'm still not thrilled. In physics there's something called "the observer effect." This concept refers to the fact that simply by observing something, one can change the outcome. I remember all of those *Star Trek* episodes where the characters had to abide by the Prime Directive—not to change or interfere in any way with less technologically advanced societies. So if crew members needed to study a certain primitive indigenous people, they had to ensure that they remained invisible and hidden at every moment. Even their very presence would have some unforeseen effect upon the people being studied. B'nei mitzvah parents would be wise to follow this procedure as well.

A parent can significantly change the dynamic in the room simply by sitting in a chair and never uttering a word. Kids will hesitate to ask or answer a question in fear of saying the wrong thing. They will be overly aware of every slight mistake they make while singing (even if the parent doesn't read or understand a word of Hebrew). And frankly, I find myself making subtle changes in my own teaching style—perhaps joking a little less or filtering every word of what I say through the lens of what I anticipate the parent will think.

## Ways to Sabotage at Home

There's one sentence that I believe all parents have said to their children. It's supposed to make them feel better and ease the stress that the kids are experiencing. When otherwise well-meaning parents see their children getting upset or nervous over the prospect of standing up in front of a couple hundred people, they *always* give the same dubiously helpful, fingernails-on-the-blackboard piece of advice:

*"It's okay to make a mistake. No one will understand what you're saying anyway."*

Sound familiar? If you're reading this, then you've probably either heard it or said it. First, this actually provides no comfort at all to a kid who really isn't looking forward to being the center of attention on the synagogue bimah, mistakes or not. Second, it's *not true*—there will be plenty of people who will notice mistakes. But third, and of the utmost importance within the context of this book: this one sentence totally encapsulates everything that is wrong and lacking in how we prepare b'nei mitzvah students. (I could actually have used it as the title.)

Let's take each item one at a time.

Even allowing for an otherwise flawless performance (maybe our bar or bat mitzvah student took one of those rabbinical b'nei mitzvah pills), there's still an incredible amount of stress involved in having to stand up and be the sole focus of hundreds of eyes. Kids that age are naturally self-conscious, ill at ease, and uncomfortable in their own skin. Some of us outgrow those things; some never do. But while the fear of making even one minor error can be all-consuming, kids will still worry and stress about their b'nei mitzvah.

Next, I know that parents are trying to be helpful. We want to protect our children and when we see them overly worried about something, we do our best to take that fear away. So we'll say almost anything to convince the kids that it won't really be as scary as they think. However, when kids are told that mistakes don't matter because no one will understand what they're saying, we are sending the exact opposite, most destructive message possible. Parents who tell this to their children are overtly saying two things: (1) None of what you're doing actually means anything. It's all a bunch of random sounds and phrases. (2) You and I—and every other Jew—have no connection to this at all, but you must recite these meaningless syllables in order to pass the test.

Then there are corollaries to this idea. Notice that the only reason why an error is permitted is that there's presumably no one present who will know the difference. (Other than the rabbi and cantor, of course, but they don't seem to worry about us.) The implied message to children then is that anyone who actually might notice a mistake will make awful, negative judgments about them. He mispronounced that word! She sang the wrong tune! Those trope melodies were incorrect!

Parents, you're not easing the pressure on your child. You're *adding* to it.

Instead, parents and teachers should communicate to students from the very beginning that of course they will make mistakes. (I've been at this job for many years, and I have yet to witness a single bar or bat mitzvah student who did not make at least one mistake.) I have my students picture the exact opposite of what their parents tell them. I tell them to imagine that the entire sanctuary is filled with the world's leading Torah scholars. They know every word, every trope, every syllable. *They* will certainly notice every mistake you make.

Now what? What will they think of you? Will they sit in quiet horror at the thought that this thirteen-year-old kid can't get through a haftarah flawlessly? Or will they understand that, in fact, it's pretty difficult for any thirteen-year-old to stand in front of people and sing (and in another language no less), and they're simply doing the best they can. And if my imaginary group of Torah scholars would comprehend this, then certainly a student's family, friends, and supporters would feel the same way, even more strongly.

### As an Aside . . .

Sometimes a mistake becomes the most endearing and memorable part of b'nei mitzvah services. When a student "messes up" a little, sometimes he can't help but giggle or smile or shoot me an "oops" look. I have had parents remind me of how their daughter—now in her thirties or forties!—lost her place and had to stop and have me help her find it. It's a funny memory now.

Mistakes bring out an individual's personality in a way that a robotic, cookie-cutter, flawless rendition could never do.

Finally, when you give your kids the "it doesn't matter" line, then you're basically writing this book for me. It's as if you, too, understand that what we're teaching kids and having them memorize by rote has no modern meaning and is of no importance other than as a required goal.

If your child were a passionate musician scheduled to perform a piano recital, no matter how nervous she was, you would never tell her that she could make a bunch of mistakes in the piece because no one would be familiar with it. Instead, you would intuitively understand that her goal would be to learn and internalize the music, to practice and prepare, and then to simply play as well as she could. Everyone in the audience would be thrilled, occasional missed note and all.

For all the "it's just a game" mentality that parents and coaches have to adopt, every athlete and parent understands that it's important to give an enormous effort on the field. Losing a game is a part of life; it's the practice, planning, and performance during the game that is most important. I can't imagine any parent telling a child before a championship match, "Don't worry, no one really cares about this game anyway."

Yet this is exactly the message that so many parents are communicating to their kids. Just get through it. It has no real meaning, and when it's over, you can forget about the whole thing.

## Parent as Personal Secretary

Let's go back to our "What's the goal?" conversation. We can put our focus group together and brainstorm all the desired outcomes of kids becoming b'nei mitzvah (in chapter 9, we'll do just that). After the usual bits about learning the service and knowing how to read the Torah, we will always get to items like "taking on more responsibility" and "becoming a Jewish adult" (whatever in the world that means). While we can make many valid arguments why a seventh or eighth grader is not really ready to embrace any definition of adulthood, we certainly can hope for some increased level of maturity and responsibility.

In the secular world, these expectations are demonstrated all the time. Kids get more homework at school. A child might be allowed to have a cell phone but has the obligation to take care of it and always keep a parent informed of where they are. It's the balance that parents, teachers, and children eternally play out—to take a lesson from Rabbi Spiderman, who understood the concept, "With great power comes great responsibility"; we know that with increasing independence come more expectations. The message to our kids: yes, we are happy to give you more leeway and privileges. But show us that you're ready to handle them.

This is played out in b'nei mitzvah lessons all the time, and parents are often the worst offenders at undermining this idea. When I see this dynamic at play it reinforces to me all over again why our arbitrary b'nei mitzvah age of thirteen has become increasingly irrelevant and downright inappropriate for this rite of passage. Not only can we not usually consider a thirteen-year-old child mature enough to be referred to as an adult (Jewish or otherwise), but parents know this as well.

In many cases, parents completely and utterly take over every aspect of b'nei mitzvah training. As much as it may seem so, this is not an indictment of parents; rather, it's a reflection or snapshot of current life. Kids' schedules are increasingly busy and complex, while one or both working parents need to coordinate who is driving where and at what time. Students have to find time to complete homework, while parents have to figure out how to get everyone home for dinner. So when I talk about this dynamic between parent and child, this isn't some grumpy old man waxing nostalgic for simpler times. (I'm neither grumpy nor old.) I actually think it's wonderful that young teens have such a variety of activities that are available throughout the year. Naturally, though, b'nei mitzvah lessons become one more drain on the family's resources.

So parents predictably go into parenting mode. Much as they would treat any activity—soccer, voice lessons, gymnastics—they take over all aspects of lessons: scheduling, homework, progress, nagging, and monitoring. As a result, they are unwittingly working against the one overarching result that we're all working toward: an increased sense of responsibility and self-sufficiency.

Let's look at a typical scenario of how many b'nei mitzvah lessons play out.

1. At some appropriate point well in advance of the date, either the rabbi or cantor will contact the parent, or the parent will proactively reach out to the temple office to inquire about scheduling lessons. After a moderate amount of juggling while everyone peers at their calendars, a specific weekly time slot is agreed upon.

2. In many cases, this will be followed by the parent explaining their child's specific needs or learning differences, or even vague apologies that their Hebrew reading is likely not as fluent as we might expect (spoiler alert: we've seen it all and are happy to work with every student).

3. The parent brings their child to the temple, walks them in, makes sure they are comfortable and not too nervous to have to begin lessons, assures them, "I'll be right back in forty-five (or thirty or sixty) minutes to get you," and leaves. Alternately, the parent waits in the lobby for the lesson to be over, or even worse, comes into the office with their child and sits through the lesson.

4. After the lesson is completed, the parent makes sure that the student has all of their folders and books and asks how it all went. The parent

then confirms that the next lesson will be the same time next week (while having calendar open) and then makes a mental or written note of the homework that I assigned during the lesson.

5. At home during the week, the parents repeatedly ask, "Did you practice?" or sometimes more disturbingly, "The cantor is going to be mad at you if you didn't practice." (No I won't.) Depending of course on the student, sometimes this aspect of training is a breeze, while other times it's a constant battle filled with fighting and crying.

6. Once in a while, the parent will contact the cantor or rabbi to tell them that we're going to skip the lesson that week. "_____ had a really busy week and just wasn't able to practice, and they're nervous that they won't be able to sing anything. I promise that next week they'll practice a lot, and we'll see you next time."

7. As the bar or bat mitzvah gets closer, the parents have made all of the necessary (and costly) arrangements. This obviously includes every aspect of the party (much more on that in chapter 8) but also refers to the service itself. Invitations, kippot, programs, honors—every facet of the bar or bat mitzvah ceremony has been perfectly orchestrated by the parents. Much like the proverbial beleaguered groom at his wedding—all the kid needs to do is show up, sing, and leave.

Clearly, we're seeing an underlying thread here. The one obvious and most attainable goal of having a young person take on a larger and more significant role in Judaism is utterly thwarted by well-meaning parents. Again, while later chapters will lay out ideas and suggestions for modestly or radically different models of b'nei mitzvah training, we can fix this problem right now—today—while still operating within the current paradigm. We don't need to change much at all.

Let's review those steps again and see how we can incorporate a level of personal responsibility and maturity.

1. The cantor and student have a conversation about upcoming b'nei mitzvah lessons. This could take place during Religious School, or the cantor could ask if the kid has an e-mail address so they can write back and forth about it. (Cc'ing the parent might be a prudent and sensible option in this case). Together, the cantor and student might discuss what the student is most excited or nervous about with lessons starting soon and what they'd like to get out of the process. They do their best to figure out a logical day and time for lessons, and then, with the parent's approval and confirmation, the lessons are set.

2. If the student is feeling particularly insecure about their reading ability, they can simply tell the cantor, "I don't think I can read Hebrew much at all." That will result in a conversation about strategies for practicing and ways to learn the material, as well as assurances that they are, in fact, in good company among the vast majority of their peers, whose Hebrew reading skills vary widely.

3. The student is dropped off at temple, walks in, and proceeds into the cantor's or rabbi's office. After the lesson, they wait at the lobby door for their ride home. Bonus: if they happen to live within a certain distance, and if the time and weather allows, the student walks or bikes to the lesson.

4. At the completion of the lesson, the student gathers up their stuff, makes sure they have everything, and is completely clear on what they have to work on for the next lesson. Perhaps the student tells the cantor that the following week they have an important event (championship game, play rehearsal, and so on) and asks if there is a way to reschedule that lesson. Together, they decide to either skip that week or find another open time slot, which the cantor writes down and the student takes home.

5. At home, the student treats bat mitzvah material as any other schoolwork.

6. On the day of the next lesson, the student e-mails to let the cantor know that they never got a chance to practice even once and asks if they should cancel the lesson because they won't know any of the new material. Alternate scenario: the student is sick—perhaps they stayed home from school that day—and e-mails the cantor that they are too sick to come to lessons. (FYI: the cantor will *always* be happy to cancel a lesson with a student who is sick.)

7. As the bat mitzvah dates gets closer, the student knows exactly which parts of the service they will lead and the content and name of the Torah portion. They have at least given their opinion on certain honors ("I'd like my best friend to come up and help me lead *Ein Keloheinu*.") and have committed to donating a certain percentage of their gift money to a charity or cause that they find personally meaningful.

Wow, what a difference. We didn't need any sweeping changes, and I didn't need to write the rest of this book. These are all differences that almost every family could make starting today.

Throughout the entire process, from before the first lesson and culminating with the ceremony itself, the one important goal of taking on more responsibility is stressed, emphasized, and reinforced. And if you tell me that some kids might be uncomfortable e-mailing or communicating with me on their own, I would respond, "That's exactly the point." If you informed me that a student's particular learning style makes it more difficult for them to decode and learn Hebrew words, I would completely understand and would want to hear the specific difficulties directly from the student so that we can work out strategies and a path forward through the material.

Parents have fallen into the habit of thinking that b'nei mitzvah lessons are exclusively about learning how to sing a haftarah and lead a service. That's why our current, and largely irrelevant, model has stopped serving the needs of our Jewish community. Instead, becoming b'nei mitzvah—whether that's utilizing our current method or embracing sweeping changes—is all about pushing the envelope and trying something that's new and uncomfortable. That's more of an indicator of growing maturity than memorizing a bunch of text that will never be repeated.

# CHAPTER SEVEN

~

# The Problems

Before we really begin to reimagine what a bar or bat mitzvah can be and all of the many options that exist, let's look closely at what may not be working for a lot of kids. Again, for some teens and families, the status quo is great. Like Sarah back in chapter 5, a child with a certain skill set and aptitude will excel at the material and have a positive experience. For every kid like Sarah, though, I suspect there are many who don't fit that pattern.

## An Age-Old Problem

If you had a time machine and the ability to go back to any age, would you *ever* return to when you were thirteen?

I didn't think so.

I once jokingly suggested that a huge committee of sadistic rabbis got together hundreds of years ago and decided to pull a fast one on the Jewish people. They found the most problematic, least desirable, and altogether inappropriate age in a kid's life and decreed that *this* would be the time when we'd make him stand up in front of every friend and relative and sing for two hours in a foreign language.

- Wait, isn't age thirteen around the time when a boy's voice starts changing? Yup, too bad.
- Wouldn't a thirteen-year-old child be self-conscious about his or her body and all of the changes that go along with it? Yes, sorry.

- Can a thirteen-year-old really process on more than a superficial level what it means to be a lifelong, involved, and committed Jew? Maybe, but probably not.
- Are many thirteen-year-old kids caught up in "middle-school drama," with shifting cliques and friendships? Oh well.
- Is a thirteen-year-old kid good at memorizing stuff? Yes! See, it's the perfect age to study and prepare for b'nei mitzvah.

As I said back in chapter 1, the age of thirteen probably made more sense at one time—for sociological and economic reasons. And just as fifty may be the new thirty-five, age thirteen feels a lot younger for kids in modern times.

### As an Aside . . .

There are, in fact, common and accepted examples of celebrating b'nei mitzvah well after the age of thirteen.

First, many synagogues will run an adult b'nei mitzvah class. Usually this is intended for those congregants who never had the opportunity, for whatever reason, to mark their roles as Jewish adults earlier in their lives. Sometimes this might include people who chose to join the Jewish religion later in life and would like to formally mark their entrance into the community. More commonly, though, there are women who came of age at a time when girls did not enjoy the same privileges and opportunities as boys. Of course I wholeheartedly welcome such participation but am eager to point out—as I've done already throughout this book—that any Jew over the age of thirteen is certainly considered bar or bat mitzvah regardless of whether they were able to celebrate or have a ceremony. Adult b'nei mitzvah is about education and recommitting—not becoming something different or undergoing a fundamental change.

Second, some older congregants will sometimes mark a "second" bar or bat mitzvah at age eighty-three. This is based on a biblical reference that a typical lifespan is seventy years. Therefore, anyone who makes it to eighty-three is enjoying a new life plus thirteen years—time to celebrate another bar mitzvah. This is another beautiful custom; anything that helps form a stronger connection to Judaism is fine with me.

### The Issue of Gender

While this issue may have always existed, it's really only recently that there would be an awareness of it as a potential problem. While schools and other institutions have made much progress towards becoming gender neutral and inclusive, the ritual of becoming b'nei mitzvah still lags far behind.

It's a formidable problem. The Hebrew language, as is the case with numerous others, utilizes gender in its grammar. All words are masculine or feminine—just look at how much effort I've tried to put into interchanging the terms bar mitzvah (masculine), bat mitzvah (feminine), and b'nei mitzvah (plural, but still literally the masculine form). Furthermore, numerous Jewish rituals themselves are based on one's gender. When we call someone up for an aliyah to the Torah, we use the Hebrew word *ya'amod* for a male and *ta'amod* for a female; both mean to stand up and step forward. All kids have a Hebrew name, and are taught to then use a parent's name after the term *ben* (son of) or *bat* (daughter of). On Friday evenings when it's traditional to offer children words of blessing, the texts are different based on whether the blessing is being delivered to a son or daughter.

How then do we address the issue of kids who are transgender or gender nonbinary, or are in the beginning process of being aware of their own identity?

There have been some attempts—some more awkward than others—to eradicate as many references to gender as possible out of the correct and appropriate desire to be sensitive to all children. Sometimes, just as has become increasingly common in English, the plural will be used universally, so that we simply use the term b'nei mitzvah as a singular word. Others have tried to skip the gender-identifying letters and only refer to each child's "b'mitzvah." (As I said, awkward.) In place of *ben* or *bat* to identify an individual as someone's son or daughter, some synagogues have started using *mi-beit*, literally "from the house of," or *mi-mishpachat*, "from the family of." These are decent solutions, but don't address the underlying problem that for kids who are possibly just taking the first steps in coming to terms with their identities, the added stress of this very public, social, and performance-based ceremony must be brutal.

## Peer Pressure

Whenever we hear this term, we immediately associate it with the way our kids (and often our teenage children) behave when surrounded by their peers. Even though they may very well know the proper thing to do or not to do, they are influenced by people around them—and this may be for a variety of reasons. The items below would perfectly apply to both kids and their parents when thinking about planning and preparing for b'nei mitzvah:

- They may want to simply do what they see everyone else doing.
- They may feel that they'll fit in better if they go along with a certain course of action.
- They're insecure about the way they think others view them and want to present another face to the public.
- They figure that if everyone else is doing something, then it must be okay.

Peer pressure is alive and well in the world of b'nei mitzvah, and both kids and their parents fall victim to it all the time. When you have a system that prescribes one accepted path to a given outcome, then do *you* want to be the one that goes against the herd? Do you want to be the parent who plans something completely different to mark this rite of passage when everyone else is having a service, complete with two hundred invited guests? How would you feel as a thirteen-year-old middle-school student who feels the need to explain over and over why their bar or bat mitzvah doesn't look like all the other ones going on among the Jewish kids?

A number of times, I have had parents tell me over the course of their child's bat mitzvah lessons that "I want my daughter to learn all of the Torah readings," or something similar to that. It's simply a statement of quantity. There is *this* much that is possible to learn, so that's what I want her to do. End of discussion.

I should point out that while it is certainly possible for a student to learn and memorize an entire Torah reading, it's not the norm. It will depend on the particular week and how long that reading is, as well as the background of the student. I have had isolated examples of extremely talented and motivated students who have pulled it off. But that honestly has nothing to do with what our parent is expressing here. When I hear "I want my daughter to learn all of the Torah readings," it almost certainly has to do with peer pressure—usually experienced by the parents themselves.

My eventual follow-up question would be a simple and politely worded, "*Why* do you want your daughter to do all of the Torah readings?"

The answer usually has to do with a misplaced motivation to take what most of the other kids are doing and exceed that amount. If they're doing A and B, then I want my daughter to do A, B, and C.

The desire may arise out of a mistaken belief that if a child does more, then the experience and quality of the bat mitzvah is increased.

Learning how to read Torah is indeed a valuable and useful skill within the world of Jewish synagogue life—no question. If a parent made it clear that it was a top priority that a student attain that skill for future opportunities to read Torah during services, I would be thrilled. But most of the all-the-Torah-reading families are those that are unlikely to appear much at all in future years. They are viewing everything through the lens of peer pressure and how an incredible performance will appear in front of their invited audience.

## Special Needs

I do not have formal educational training in special education. Yet I am routinely called upon to tutor kids with special needs and learning differences. Often the parents will tell me that their child must deal with a specific problem in order to call my attention to it, and then we might discuss how lessons will go.

This particular issue is really upsetting to me. We might be talking about a kid with a minor learning difference or one that has profound special needs. In all cases, we proceed pretty much the way we do with every student. Lessons once a week, drilling and memorizing skills, words, and melodies—what may differ is how that memorization takes place and the amount of material that we're expecting to cover. Because of our b'nei mitzvah assembly line and because virtually all kids are on the exact same path, the parents of children who have specific issues and needs insist that their kid prepare for and learn the same material. Of course they do. How could they act any differently? Any alteration in the accepted path would only call more attention to their child's learning difference or capabilities, and would exacerbate an already stressful situation. It's so much easier to plug every child into the same template.

It then falls upon us—the Jewish professionals—to make some kind of assessment about how much we think the kid can learn. And we have to do it almost immediately; we can't spend seven out of nine months of b'nei mitzvah training struggling and ultimately failing to learn a haftarah, only to make a last-minute decision to master another text. We have to decide almost first thing: "I think we should not aim to learn haftarah. Let's start with Torah instead. And these pages in the siddur will be too hard, so I'd like to focus instead on these other pages." So now we have a student and family that already feels different and marginalized. One could frame these decisions by saying that we are indeed making every effort to tailor the bar or bat mitzvah service according to each kid's abilities. But when 99 percent of the students are learning one fixed set of material, how must that poor 1 percent feel? Sorry, your kid is different so we have to proceed in another direction.

Furthermore, there's no evaluation of how any child with special needs processes the act of becoming a bar or bat mitzvah. Again, the one, overarching goal is not only to get through the service, but to do it in the one way that every other student, all the families, and indeed members of the congregation expect.

Don't underestimate the immense peer pressure that this produces. When preparing a child with specific needs, even when everything goes smoothly and with the complete support of the parents, not everyone gets it. There have been repeated instances when we have made an appropriate decision to scale back the scope of what a particular child will learn and sing in front of the congregation. And after the service is over, with the student having sung everything well, I will get comments from congregants and other kids asking "Why didn't he do the haftarah?" "How come he got to do so little?" And the inevitable, "Wow, that must have a been a tough one to teach." Sure, you'll find insensitive people everywhere no matter how inclusive and aware a given congregation is. But this will always be a problem when you have one set, approved, and expected way for every single Jewish child to learn. On the other hand, if each child's b'nei mitzvah experience was radically different, kids wouldn't be evaluated and measured against each other.

## Interfaith Families

Certainly an entire second book could be written on nothing more than the implications of interfaith marriage.

### As an Aside . . .

I much prefer using the word "interfaith" rather than "intermarriage." To me, the latter term is condescending, implying that the two people in the marriage are profoundly different from each other or that the Jewish spouse is inherently superior. On the other hand, "interfaith" accurately refers to the presence of more than one religion. Of course, it would be better altogether to stop needing to label people in the first place, but that's probably a topic for that second book.

I won't point out all the ways that Judaism puts a stumbling block in front of interfaith families to become full and involved members of the Jewish community. But one aspect of this important issue has a direct connection to our topic. The entire b'nei mitzvah machine revolves around a worship service—leading prayers and chanting a haftarah or Torah reading. By its very definition, it excludes a non-Jewish parent or other close family members. I discussed this in some detail back in chapter 5. Of course, the degree to which this is true will vary greatly throughout congregations and the various movements that are more or less accepting of interfaith families. But simply put, Jews pray one way and non-Jews pray another. Because the one and only focus of the b'nei mitzvah service is *prayer*—well, you can see how this is automatically a problem for the non-Jewish family member.

This also places an added burden upon the child in an interfaith family. Because the bar or bat mitzvah ceremony has become uniform, anything that departs from that norm is looked upon with a negative light.

Let's imagine Max, a soon-to-be bar mitzvah boy. Throughout much of the year, Max has been attending his friends' b'nei mitzvah services in his own and neighboring synagogues. He notices a similar pattern. During the Torah service, there are numerous honors that are handed out to relatives and friends. So Max notices a lot of his friends' relatives taking part in the service—opening and closing the ark, lifting the Torah, and having an aliyah. One of the emotional highlights of the Torah service is when both parents are called up, so that they share the bimah with the clergy and their child.

Now it's Max's turn—his bar mitzvah day has arrived. But for his service, something is different. Max's parents are interfaith—his mother is Jewish and his father is not. Still, they have made the decision to maintain a Jewish household, affiliate with a temple, and send Max to Religious School. While there may have been some differences or conflicts, they were always under the radar and never affected Max in a direct way. Now, however, the fact of Max's interfaith family is on full and frontal display. As is the case in a lot of Conservative synagogues, most honors and aliyot may only be given to Jewish people. This perhaps make sense when thinking about the function of aliyot in the Torah service. Each person recites a blessing thanking God for the gift of Torah. In most congregations, the text specifically praises God for choosing the Jews from all the other nations. Strictly speaking, even if a non-Jewish person could recite the Hebrew words (and in fact they're almost always provided in transliteration), they wouldn't make sense in context. But this fact shouldn't preclude a non-Jewish parent from coming up and standing next to a Jewish spouse who would be reciting the words. Still, in many cases, the non-Jewish parent may not even ascend the bimah during the aliyah.

In any case, during the service, only half of Max's family is really visible—his mother's side. They are the ones coming up to take part in the Torah service and be called to the Torah. And most strikingly, only Max's mother gets called up for an aliyah. Her father—not Jewish—must remain seated and can only look on. Sure, there may be a couple lower-tier honors reserved for non-Jewish honorees, but they take place at a less intense part of the service.

So Max, through no fault of his own, and after having done "everything right," now feels different and somewhat marginalized. He may not be able to articulate the reasons for his feelings, but they will likely remain with him as his view of how he connected to Judaism.

When we speak of reimagining the way that we prepare our kids to become b'nei mitzvah, we have to keep the big picture in mind. It's not simply a matter of the material that we emphasize or the timetable that might be appropriate for that child. We can't state that we want that individual to form an adult relationship with Judaism and at the same time create conflicts within the family. Instead, we need to embrace a more holistic view—understanding that no one and nothing exists in a vacuum. If we teach Max a bunch of material and have him recite it flawlessly on the day of his bar mitzvah, but without any regard to how this will affect his family or their feelings, then we haven't accomplished much at all.

As we go forward throughout this book, let's consider each new idea, each suggestion as something that will work not just for each child, but for everyone in the family. We need to respect the needs and distinct personalities of each bar or bat mitzvah kid as well as their families.

# CHAPTER EIGHT

~

# The Party

I love a party—who doesn't? Whether it's a small, intimate gathering or a lavish affair held at a formal venue, parties and celebrations are a wonderful way to enjoy company and see friends and relatives that you may not get to see on a regular basis because they live far away.

The Bar Mitzvah Party is a category unto itself—alternately steeped in 1970s-era, wide lapel nostalgia or lycra-clad dancing girls that you can watch again and again on YouTube. Our pop culture is filled with depictions of over-the-top parties, with countless scenes taking place on various television shows and movies.

Normally, I wouldn't even think to include a chapter like this in a book about b'nei mitzvah preparation. Throughout my career, my approach has always been to steer clear of this domain and deal exclusively with the religious and educational aspects of training. Anything related to the party and everything that goes along with it—guest list, venue, theme, as well as paying for the whole thing—I gladly stay out of and leave to the family.

But in thinking further about it, I've come to realize that the party is, in fact, a substantial part of this rite of passage and we'd be ill-advised to ignore it. In many cases, the celebration has utterly overshadowed any other aspect of the bar or bat mitzvah. The service is seen as the required, put-your-head-down-and-get-it-done part of the occasion, after which the real event can take place. Family members and guests file into the sanctuary, clearly uncomfortable and tentative in unfamiliar surroundings. Many have no real idea what's going on—often including the b'nei mitzvah family themselves—and are content to watch the nervous thirteen-year-old make their way through the action. Finally, after an interminable two or so hours, the service comes to an end and everyone can now begin the real act of celebrating, as they seem to stage a frenzied evacuation of the synagogue and make their way to the party.

And even with all that, I understand that it's a rare opportunity to get everyone—grandparents, extended family, distant friends—together under one roof. Families are right to seize on this moment to celebrate with each other and create more memories together. But in many cases, the form that these celebrations take is troubling—subtly or explicitly sending the wrong message and highlighting false aspects of what the bar or bat mitzvah really means.

If we're going to embark on ways to raise the bar for our students, and to reimagine what and how our kids approach this significant rite of passage, shouldn't we also look at the whole picture? The celebration is certainly an extension of the day, and we can encompass it into our new way of thinking as well.

## The Illusion of Adulthood

How many times over the last hundred or so years has some well-meaning adult—rabbi, parent, uncle, middle-school friend—said these words to a bar mitzvah boy:

"You're a man now!"

Most b'nei mitzvah parties then take this concept and expand on it. We take a thirteen-year-old kid and make him the sole focus of an adult (and often adult-themed) party. In many cases, a typical b'nei mitzvah party more closely resembles a wedding—and the price point is in the ballpark as well. There's lots of drinking, formal attire, live bands, toasts, and heavy meals (would you like the prime rib or the salmon?).

All of this to honor a middle-school kid?

## Happy Birthday

Assuming we're holding on to the current model of b'nei mitzvah, the occasion marks the time when a young Jewish person turns thirteen according to the Jewish calendar and is now eligible to participate fully in the rituals and traditions of the Jewish religion. That's it. Full stop. I've said it multiple times already: nothing magical happens to a child at the ceremony. There's no transformation that occurs from the time the service starts until it's over, a couple of hours later. Rather, it acknowledges the fact that a young person has *already* become bar or bat mitzvah simply as a result of reaching a certain age according to the Jewish calendar.

### As an Aside . . .

There's something that makes me more than a little uncomfortable about the "You're a man now" cliché. It sits just above an unseen layer of toxic masculinity, as if to say that there's one accepted way that men should act. What does it actually mean? If a boy became upset at school and started crying, would a teacher say, "Hey, you're a man now!" There are so many connotations that exist in that statement that are routinely placed in a young boy's head. I remember watching a movie—one of those ubiquitous bar mitzvah party scenes that I referred to—where the bar mitzvah boy, upon being told he was a man now, proceeded to grab the twenty-something dancer and kiss her on the lips. Everyone was supposed to find that hilarious—and I imagine many did. But indeed, this is *exactly* what we're communicating when we roll out this destructive and anachronistic trope.

Similarly, we typically send the same message to young girls by making them adopt the persona of older, mature adults. I have seen so many photo shoots depicting an otherwise typical seventh-grade girl in outright sexual and provocative poses—as if we're saying, "You're a woman now! This is what you should look like." Parents will then routinely post these pictures on social media for the world to see, and the typical comments follow: "She's gorgeous!" "Stunning!!" "What a beauty!"

In both cases, we're reinforcing tired and downright inappropriate gender stereotypes.

While I've made it clear throughout this book that I take issue with the entire notion of a thirteen-year-old child being considered an adult in any context, at least one might say, "You're a Jewish adult now!" It's not perfect, but it works a little better.

Put in general terms then, a bar or bat mitzvah is really nothing more than a fancy birthday celebration. Why shouldn't the celebration that marks this special birthday be age-appropriate? I think it's a wonderful idea to plan a thirteenth birthday party for one's son or daughter. But I wonder why this would need to be a black-tie event featuring a vodka bar. Over the years, of course, I have seen every possible kind of party, and to be sure I'm really only mentioning those that are of a particular (but common) variety. There have also been some wonderful, kid-based examples, such as the parents arranging for their child to invite all of her friends for a special night out at the theater or some other fun activity and meal that would be enjoyed by a large group of middle-school kids.

## As an Aside . . .

If you ever want to get a clear snapshot of how the general public views a certain subject, look no further than the greeting card aisle at your local supermarket. Here we find every tired and clichéd theme emphasized with cute illustrations. You'll come across the lazy father who only wants to be left alone to watch TV on Father's Day, the beleaguered mother who might blessedly get one day off from cooking for everyone on Mother's Day, and every variation on how our bodies are slowly falling apart each time we celebrate a birthday.

Bar and bat mitzvah cards are no exception, and it's very telling that even the world around us has figured out what we often refuse to see or acknowledge. Consider this actual example of a bar mitzvah card that I came across:

Written in a whimsical font, the front reads, "Yada yada yada Bar Mitzvah yada yada yada Proud of You yada yada yada Mazel Tov yada yada yada."

Open it up and you see, "Just hitting the highlights so you can get on with the party."

It might have been at this precise moment when I decided that I needed to write this book.

## The Wrong Message

Put simply, b'nei mitzvah parties have a sex problem.

Somewhere along the line, someone conflated the themes of adulthood with sexuality and imbued all aspects of the celebration with inappropriate elements. Parents are rightly concerned with their kids' exposure to unsuitable images online or their temptation to share certain pictures or messages by text. They monitor (or at least try to monitor) what their kids watch and seek to send the right messages of mutual respect and age-appropriate behavior. And then the bar mitzvah party starts and our once childlike thirteen-year-old is instantly transformed into a twenty-something frat boy with everyone in attendance looking on approvingly. Young, lithe dancers dressed in tight outfits gyrate their way all over the dance floor, and in many cases, accompany the bar mitzvah boy into the hall for his first entrance—often arm in arm on either side.

Why exactly has this become a routine part of a bar mitzvah celebration?

## Cookie-Cutter Parties

B'nei mitzvah parties have the same problem as b'nei mitzvah services. In many cases, they've just become cookie-cutter affairs, indistinguishable from all of the others that occurred in past weeks.

Let's take a look at a typical bar or bat mitzvah party. If you've been to one lately, you can let me know how many of the following items I got right:

- It takes place in a fancy hall or hotel.
- There is a special area for the kids (and did you remember socks for the girls?).
- Cocktail hour for the adults begins the affair.
- Grandfather makes the motzi. (One day, the heavens will come crashing down and the earth will actually stop spinning on its axis when a family asks the *grandmother* to make the motzi.)
- It includes the necessary and required five-to-ten minutes of hora (extra points to the band singer if *v'nismicha* is pronounced correctly).
- Every member of the family hoisted up on chairs one after the other.
- First course: salads. Hurry up and get back to your seats because they will be taken away soon.
- More dancing—and you have to at least stand by the dance floor because the music is so loud it's impossible to stay seated and engage in conversation.
- Please find your seats because it's time for the montage.
- Second course: prime rib or salmon. There's a vegetarian option too, but it's so vile you should eat around the salmon.
- The kids get their own food (e.g., chicken fingers and fries) and everyone secretly wants what they're having.
- Dad gives a toast. Tears are shed.
- Coffee and dessert are brought out, giving 90 percent of the guests the signal that it's okay to leave.
- The kids have been bored since they saw pictures of themselves during the montage, but it's only 10:30 pm and they told their parents to pick them up at 11:00. Some have been hanging out together in the bathrooms and the security guy on duty has had to break them up a couple times.
- Kids pick up their goody bags with swag and leave. They will all wear the T-shirt or sweatshirt on Monday at school (which also makes it clear to the entire public school student body exactly who was and wasn't invited to this party).

Did I miss anything? I submit to you that I accurately described a high percentage of all b'nei mitzvah parties. As the saying goes, it's funny because it's true.

Now multiply that by every single child in the b'nei mitzvah class at temple—the same basic party with the same routine week after week. Many of the kids attend each other's parties (except for the ones who are left out— that's another topic) and, similarly, all of the parents who are together in this peer group are there as well. Throughout the year, each set of parents will take their own turn in hosting (and paying for) what's basically an identical party. When the year is over, everyone has the same collection of colorful plastic hats, beads, oversized sunglasses, and the strip of four vertical photo booth pictures.

What would happen if we visited this b'nei mitzvah class and all of their parents in about ten years or so—when the kids have just recently graduated from college—and asked them what they remember from all of the parties they attended during this b'nei mitzvah year. Would they be able to recollect much from one party to the next? Is there anything related to Judaism that sticks out from the celebration, or is it all a homogenous haze of music, cocktails, DJs, dancers, and party favors? (I do imagine that they're fully cognizant of the immense amount of money they spent and what that amount might have looked like ten years later thanks to compound interest.)

This "sameness" of parties itself sends the wrong message. It is telling everyone that there is nothing unique about each individual (other than whatever theme you can turn into centerpieces for the tables). The entire experience—from first lesson all the way through to coffee and dessert—is simply a one-path assembly line with no room for other options. After all, a conveyer belt only moves toward one location—there are no opportunities to diverge.

The other insidious message is that this particular thirteen-year-old child is the center of the universe. When we attend a wedding, we rightly focus solely on the couple—making them the center of our attention and lavishing our emotions and praise upon them. At b'nei mitzvah parties, we do the same thing to middle-school kids who memorized some melodies and put on an uncomfortable suit or dress. In my life, I have never met any seventh grader—and that includes my own two incredible children that I will be happy to endlessly brag about—that are worthy of this level of praise, attention, and adulation at this stage of their life.

## Value-Based Message

Elsewhere in this book, we embark on a deep dive into the issue of goals. We ask ourselves, What are we truly trying to accomplish with b'nei mitzvah preparation and the ceremony? And we identify many such examples of what we'd like our b'nei mitzvah kids to take with them—both immediately and in the long run—after the ceremony is over.

But right here and right now, I'm sure that we can agree on one important message that we feel that every single bar or bat mitzvah student should embrace as a lifelong goal: Living a life of Jewish value. Of course, that can and should carry myriad meanings—there's no one single Jewish value. We teach many such ideals, such as giving *tzedakah*, having compassion for the less fortunate, and the notion of *tikkun olam* (fixing the world). This last term is purposely vague so that it may be meaningfully interpreted by the greatest number of people.

I feel strongly that the celebration of a bar or bat mitzvah should carry as much import as the ceremony itself. There is a jarring disconnect when a young person talks about their community service project ("I helped less-privileged kids with their homework after school." "I collected backpacks for less-fortunate school kids.") and then makes his way to a lavish affair that has absolutely no connection to any aspect of Judaism. (And no, having the band play a hora for five minutes doesn't count.)

My point is that the current b'nei mitzvah model has evolved into two separate and discrete entities that have nothing to do with each other: the Before, which includes all lessons, preparation and the service itself; and the After, which involves the party, and then often the after-party, brunch for out-of-town guests, and so forth. There is usually no connection between the Before and the After.

In thinking about reimagining what it means to be b'nei mitzvah, one needs to think about the party too. One of the most common questions a family will ask when beginning to plan for the party is "What's the theme?" But in fact, every bar or bat mitzvah party already has a theme: Judaism. In the next section of the book, we'll get into lots of specifics about ways that kids can approach this rite of passage that may be similar to what we're already doing, or may differ radically from the well-worn path. In any case, one can and should structure the celebration to be an extension of the ceremony.

## As an Aside . . .

I'm putting this brief discussion here, in a sidebar, because I don't want to focus on it needlessly and distract from the larger subject.

I'd like to pose the controversial question: Is it actually appropriate in any way, Jewishly or otherwise, to spend a five- or six-figure amount on a bar or bat mitzvah celebration?

There are two distinct groups that we can consider—those that can easily afford this amount and those who really can't but find ways to come up with the money. In either case, might we consider better ways to devote those huge sums? A key part of b'nei mitzvah preparation is accomplishing some activity related to social action or performing a mitzvah of some kind. Some families will even earmark a certain percentage of the monetary gifts toward a Jewish cause. All of that is appropriate and praiseworthy. But I can't help but identify a disconnect between making a token (or even more substantial) gift to a worthy Jewish cause and then spending many tens of thousands of dollars (or more!) on a five-hour party.

I want to make it clear that, as much as it may seem otherwise, I am not passing judgment on the way that other people choose to celebrate or spend their money. I'm questioning the context of that expenditure.

PART III

~

# WHERE WE CAN BE

# CHAPTER NINE

~

# The Reimagining

This chapter will be the fun part of the book.

How often do you get the opportunity to take an institution—something that is anchored (one might say mired) in tradition and utterly create it over again from scratch?

The only rule for this chapter is that there are no rules. Nothing is off the table. You're allowed to consider subtle or minor changes along with groundbreaking suggestions that would render the current model of b'nei mitzvah training and ceremonies unrecognizable.

Let's pretend that we are at a corporate retreat, and our session will be to visualize and create an appropriate rite of passage for young Jews. I will be your moderator and I've already positioned myself at the front of the room next to the whiteboard. I'm ready to hear all of your suggestions.

## Goals Goals Goals

Before we can really proceed on what, how, when, or even if such a milestone can be properly acknowledged, I have to ask the same questions that have reverberated throughout this entire book: What are you trying to accomplish? What are your intended goals of b'nei mitzvah?

Clearly, we have now seen that there is no single answer that will apply to every family or individual. Furthermore, we will proceed under the assumption that any goal you come up with is just as valid as anyone else's. We won't make any judgments based on someone's level of religious knowledge, observance, or involvement. Great, I already see some hands up—as you shout out your responses I'll write them down on the board:

- Learn to read Torah and do a haftarah
- Become more involved in the Jewish community
- Lead services
- Become a Jewish adult
- Learn more about and form a stronger connection with Israel
- Understand Jewish history, especially the Holocaust
- Know a set of well-known Hebrew or Jewish songs
- Be able to feel comfortable in services anywhere in the world
- Learn trope
- Get experience with standing up and speaking in front of a crowd
- Learn the meaning and message of a Torah portion
- Know how the Jewish calendar works
- Do the same thing that all the other kids are doing at that age
- Be the first girl in the family to have a bat mitzvah
- Make the grandparents happy
- Be able to read Hebrew
- Take on an increased level of responsibility
- Become proficient with a Saturday-morning service
- Fulfill a requirement of being Jewish
- Feel a sense of accomplishment at working so hard on something
- Have an occasion to bring the entire extended family together for a celebration
- Instill a sense of pride in being Jewish
- Form a connection with Israel
- Learn Jewish values
- Become more mature
- Become a Jewish leader

Wow, that was a lot of responses—thanks to everyone for participating! In looking at the wide variety of goals that people provided, I think we can recognize that many of them fall within certain categories. So let me divide up all of the possible goals into a few distinct areas, and put your answers into the appropriate place:

**Religious Growth/Worship Experience**
- Torah portion
- Services

- Trope
- Reading Torah and haftarah
- Jewish calendar
- Comfort in services at any synagogue
- Jewish songs
- Read Hebrew

## Personal Growth/Increased Maturity and Responsibility

- Jewish adult
- More mature
- Increased level of responsibility
- Public speaking
- More involved in Jewish community
- A first for a girl in family
- Sense of accomplishment
- Jewish leader
- Jewish values

## Cultural/Ethnic Identification

- Stronger connection with Israel
- Jewish history
- Knowledge of Holocaust
- Join with rest of age group in recognized ceremony
- Fulfill requirement
- Pride in being Jewish

## Other?

- Make the grandparents happy
- Bring the whole family together

This is truly a wonderful set of goals—each one of them is worthy and admirable. Many of these goals are in fact achieved within our existing model of b'nei mitzvah training. Even if a family's priorities differ (for instance, less of a religious motivation and more of a cultural one), many of these items will be addressed along the way. That's one reason why we are stuck with the status quo—it works just enough to make most people think they've achieved all of the important goals.

Furthermore, notice how so many of the suggested goals differ wildly. While some parents would be thrilled if their daughter became proficient at reading Torah (because they knew the opportunity would arise again and again), other parents would be more than satisfied with having their son simply having a positive connection with his Jewish identity without worrying so much about specific skills. And others would be happy merely having a joyous occasion to gather the whole family. As we reimagine what a bar or bat mitzvah might entail, we can aim to tailor the process to each family's goals. Or to put it more bluntly: Why waste months of Jewish educational time teaching a kid to do something that the family readily admits will likely never happen again?

So now let me erase my whiteboard and start with something new. I want to ask all of you some deeper questions—and you have to promise that you'll answer honestly and sincerely. As I might tell a class full of elementary kids: Don't give me the answers that you think I want to hear. Say what's really on your mind.

Here goes:

- Do you truly believe that your thirteen-year-old child is fully capable of understanding what it means to be a member of the Jewish people?
- Do you honestly care whether or not your child ever reads Torah or leads a service again?
- Is attending services something that will ever be a regular routine?
- Did you join the temple because you assumed you were expected to?
- If you had your way, what would you have your child learn about Judaism?
- Are you confident that the large sum of money that you're (likely) spending for this occasion is well spent?
- Are you secretly dreading the whole process?

In reading this set of questions, you may feel that I'm leading you—that there are inherent biases built into the way I asked them. Perhaps. But I prefaced them with the direction not to answer the way you think I want to hear. For instance, if I ask if you truly believe your child is capable in taking on the role of a mature Jewish person, and you can answer "Yes!" then that's great. Parts of the current training model would be appropriate for you. But at the same time you can acknowledge that many thirteen-year-old kids are struggling emotionally and intellectually and may simply not be ready for that next stage.

Instead of taking every single child and fitting them into a prefabricated model, why can't we build the process around them? Whether you are satisfied with the way things are currently done, or you would imagine a sweeping change—wouldn't it be a refreshing step for the synagogue professional staff to initiate a conversation to ask you what your desired outcome was? Your expectations may be unrealistic or out of the realm of possibility for that synagogue—but at least it would result in a back-and-forth dialogue instead of the usual:

Here's your bar mitzvah date.
Here's when lessons start.
Here's the material that must be learned.
Here's the list of responsibilities that you will have to fulfill for the service.

And now that we've begun the process of brainstorming, it becomes hard to stop. Once you grasp the concept that literally everything you've always thought had to proceed in a certain way is in fact up for discussion, it becomes freeing.

## Turn the Question Around

Now I propose another step. You—parent or synagogue professional—become the moderator and conduct your own focus group—but with your own children and students. Ask them the same questions, and make it clear that you're really interested in what they have to say, and you're not expecting any one set of answers.

Here are some possible ways to start the discussion:

- What are the ways that make you feel connected to being Jewish?
- Do you think you'll do anything differently in the year following your bar or bat mitzvah? In the five years following?
- How do you feel about leading a service and reading Torah in front of everyone you know?
- If I said that your family could take the $XX,000 (or $XXX,000!) that you might spend on this bar or bat mitzvah and use it for something related in any way to Judaism, what suggestion could you come up with?
- As a thirteen-year-old individual, do you feel ready for this? If you had your way, would you change the age at which you accomplished this?

## Our Mission Statement

Let's build on our whiteboard brainstorming session and decide that there's one overarching goal that everyone can agree on. We'll call this our B'nei Mitzvah Mission Statement. By design, it should be general and open to various interpretations.

*Every Jewish person should find an appropriate way to mark their formal con-nection to the Jewish people.*

Most people would read that sentence and conclude that it's so vague as to be almost meaningless. Instead, I view it as a verbal Rorschach test; each reader will interpret its meaning in a different way based on their own thoughts and emotions. Seen this way, it's a perfect metaphor that we can use to "raise the bar" and reimagine how we prepare kids for their b'nei mitzvah.

Like our Talmudic ancestors, let's engage in an exegetical exercise: we'll take several words from the seemingly simple sentence above, and expand on their meaning to show how we can view things differently.

## Raising the Bar

There have been a number of references in this book so far about whether the age of thirteen is really appropriate in modern times for this rite of pas-sage. And each time, it may strike a dissonant chord. Of all the changes that I have or will suggest, perhaps the most striking and remarkable one is to abandon the well-established, seemingly rigid "rule" that dictates that all of this must happen when a Jewish youth turns thirteen.

In fact, there are other seemingly entrenched transitions that occur at a certain age that don't necessarily have to happen. For instance, many of us remember being teenagers and wanting nothing more in life than to be able to drive. We couldn't wait until that magical time (age sixteen or seventeen) when one would finally be eligible for a license and the amaz-ing changes that it would bring. A lot of us went for our driving tests on the first day we were able, often the birthday itself.

Today, things are different. Unthinkable to our generation, a lot of teens have little or no interest in driving. They know it's something they have to do, but might not be in any rush. Maybe they'll knock out the license before college, or perhaps not at all, figuring on a life in an urban, car-free setting or depending on Uber when necessary. Looking ahead to a not-so-distant future, self-driving cars may obviate the entire process for successive generations anyway.

As much as I could never personally understand such a mindset, I have to acknowledge that these teens have made a thoughtful choice:

There is something that many people do at a certain time.

It is not a priority to me right now.

I plan to do it at a later time, when I'm more motivated, and can envi-sion utilizing the skill in a certain way.

Even as a thought exercise, why can't we treat the process of becoming b'nei mitzvah in a similar fashion?

**Jewish:** Rather than being the most basic word in the sentence (or even this book), it's actually fraught with complications. For many of us, there's no doubt as to what we mean when we describe ourselves or others as Jewish. Others might view themselves as culturally Jewish with no connection to any religious aspect. And what about kids with parents who are interfaith—perhaps they identify as Jewish only to be told by Jewish professionals or other congregants that they're not truly Jewish.

### As an Aside . . .

Traditional Jewish law recognizes the concept of matrilineal descent. That is, if the mother is Jewish, then all children born to her are also Jewish, regardless of the father's faith or religion. Other branches of Judaism, however, also recognize patrilineal descent as well, so that if either parent is Jewish, then the child is considered Jewish.

This discrepancy can have far-reaching consequences. According to *halacha*, Jewish law, the child of a Jewish father and non-Jewish mother must be formally converted to Judaism. What happens when such a family that is actively and happily involved in a Reform congregation decide to relocate to another city where the only valid option for synagogue affiliation is a Conservative congregation? Do the kids get b'nei mitzvah dates? Are they required to go through the formal process of conversion—something that might be deeply offensive to a family that had always identified as Jewish until they were told that they're not, in fact, authentic Jews?

There's no one answer to this problem, and to be sure, Jewish leaders and professionals of every denomination are acutely aware of how modern Jewry is impacted. While a full discussion of interfaith marriage and family life is certainly beyond the scope of this book, we definitely have to be aware of how it affects a significant percentage of b'nei mitzvah families.

**Appropriate:** This is the entire point of this book. While one model of b'nei mitzvah training might be fine and appropriate for some kids, we need to find various options for many other students. Furthermore, the word "appropriate" may refer not only to *what* they learn, but also *why, how, when,* and *from whom.*

**Formal:** We could also substitute the word "official" in here. We don't necessarily need a huge ceremony or orchestrated service in temple. There's no requirement that a certain group of friends or relatives be present, or that it be officiated by clergy. But the idea is to at least have some line of demarcation—*here* is the moment when this rite of passage took place.

**Connection:** For some, this will take the form of involvement in synagogue, learning and leading the liturgy of the prayer book. But other ways to connect with Judaism might be secular in nature—learning academic subjects, engaging in charitable activities, or adding to the body of Jewish art or music. Right now, most Jewish families are expected to focus solely on one path of Jewish connection.

**People:** This can be interpreted in both a micro and macro way. While those families who belong to a synagogue might immediately connect more with their fellow congregants, others may seek a bond with Jews from around the country or the world. There's no single, correct way to define "The Jewish People," and one's view will likely change and evolve over time. An effective way to approach b'nei mitzvah training is to set the stage for individuals to relate to Judaism in a way that makes the most sense to them at that moment—not simply the way that rabbis and cantors say it should be.

## Beginning the Discussion

Let's consider a scenario and see if we can do some reimagining.

Leah is a typical twelve-year-old girl. She's in seventh grade at the local middle school, and her parents belong to the local synagogue. She's had her bat mitzvah date on the calendar since it was assigned by the temple three years ago. She attends religious school and her family makes limited appearances in services—mostly surrounding class events or other set occasions.

Some of her classmates have just begun lessons, while a few have already celebrated their b'nei mitzvah. When it's Leah's turn to begin, she tells her parents that she doesn't want to have a bat mitzvah. She just doesn't feel ready.

So far, of course, this is such a typical scenario—including our stressed-out twelve-year-old girl—accurately representing a substantial percentage of Jewish homes.

What comes next? You could undoubtedly write the script yourself. In many cases, our scenario would proceed like this—we'll label it the Likely Scenario.

### The Likely Scenario

Leah's parents respond to her ambivalence by assuming that all kids feel that way when faced with having a bat mitzvah. They assure her that of course she's ready and that she'll do a wonderful job, and her nervousness is completely normal. The rabbi and cantor love working with kids and they'll never get mad about practicing or making mistakes in singing or reading.

After this conversation, Leah is reassured but still feels uneasy. But her parents have made it clear—and she knows by seeing what each of her peers is going through—that this is the path she has to travel.

I'll stop describing this scenario at this point because it will just repeat much of what I've laid out throughout the rest of this book. Leah will memorize, recite, and sing her way through the material that she is given by her cantor and rabbi, and will eventually feel great relief that she was able to get through it so well. She will then return to her regular middle-school life already in progress.

### Another Scenario

Leah's parents make an unexpected move: they ask Leah *why* she doesn't feel ready to have a bat mitzvah.

This scenario could now progress into a multitude of different directions as Leah responds in any number of possible ways:

- I can't picture myself getting up and singing in front of all those people.
- I don't really believe in God.
- Everyone says that having a bat mitzvah means that you're an adult now, and I don't feel like an adult (or even more compelling: I don't want to be an adult yet).
- I just don't find learning about the service very interesting.
- I've been playing soccer/taking piano/doing gymnastics/[insert activity here] since I was five years old and I won't have as much time for that anymore. By the time I'm done with lessons, I will have missed a lot of practice/playtime.
- I'm the only Jewish kid in my class at school, and I don't want to feel so different from everyone else.
- Dad and his family are not Jewish, and I'm afraid that they'll be left out or that I'm doing something that they don't approve of.
- I've heard how much the party costs, and I'm afraid of spending all that money.

Of course, there may be additional reasons why Leah is resisting the idea of a traditional bat mitzvah that she is either unable or unwilling to articulate. Perhaps she is uncomfortable with being labeled a "bat" mitzvah girl but feels that there are no gender-nonspecific options. It's possible that the social aspect of the party presents an unbearable burden to her—having to negotiate guest lists and school cliques. In Leah's mind, it would be so much easier and make a great deal more sense to simply avoid or postpone this entire ordeal.

Another option would be to change the model altogether.

Leah is just one imaginary bat mitzvah girl, so we can't actually ask her the proper questions. But if she were here, we might begin a discussion—at her level, meeting her where she is—about her specific concerns, and then aim to elicit her thoughts on what she might like to do. This is not to say that we assume all seventh-grade kids should be put in charge of their own educational and religious upbringing. After all, we don't give our kids the choice of whether or not they want to attend school or do homework. But it's appropriate to bring them into the discussion and find out what means the most to them. The usual responses to the types of concerns that Leah expressed fall into the category of reassure and resume: "Yes, it's totally normal to be nervous." "You'll do a great job!" "It'll be okay—you'll get through it."

Instead, another strategy to address Leah's statements is to reassure and *reimagine*.

I usually cringe whenever anyone mentions the idea of giving someone "ownership" over a process, but I can't think of a better concept in this case. If Leah, along with her parents and perhaps the synagogue professionals, were to discuss and problem solve together, she would feel much more in control of the entire thing.

If I had Leah and her parents in my office, I would seek to find out specifically what she was apprehensive about. I would turn Leah's negative responses:

"I don't believe in God."

"I'm bored with Hebrew school."

"I'm too nervous to sing in front of people."

into positive questions:

"What do you love to do?"

"What's your favorite subject?"

"What do you think is the perfect age to form a connection to Judaism?"

There are now too many possibilities to list. But this is the beginning of a road map for further learning and connection that will mean something to Leah—and that she has had the opportunity to be involved with forming. The key component of this conversation is not dismissing the idea of a bat mitzvah out of hand, but rather to begin a new plan with specific goals. We could decide to check back in with each other within a month or two. Together we could create certain goals with a schedule—some independent reading, writing, or composing. I would ask Leah how and when she could envision sharing her work with her community.

I began this chapter by stating that this would be the fun part of the book. We get to take a kid like Leah—a typical, insecure, and questioning twelve- or thirteen-year-old—and have the opportunity to find out what makes her excited. Those who hesitate to make any changes at all are quick to point out that this is a crucial age to make connections and plant the seed for Jewish adulthood, but what better way can there be to accomplish that than to tap into what kids are passionate about? Having a substantive and meaningful conversation with a student and her parents and finding a way that they want to connect with the Jewish religion in a way that resonates with them—that's not only vital to our future. That's fun.

# CHAPTER TEN

~

# The Tracks

Imagine an educational system where kids are taught nothing but math. Oh sure, there might be some other assorted subjects thrown in once in a while—some English, a little history, maybe some chemistry—but for the most part students are immersed in math. They memorize formulas, drill exercises, and watch their teachers solve complicated equations and problems. This goes on through high school. When it comes time for college, all of the students continue their math education by taking all math-related courses, finally graduating with a degree in math. Whether or not that would appeal to students is beside the point.

Thankfully, the educational system is not set up that way. Of course children learn a wide variety of subjects throughout their years of school. But even as older teens, when they attend college, they continue along the same lines.

It's perfectly reasonable and expected that a high-school senior will have some idea of what they want to study at a university. While often not required right away, kids are asked to declare a "major," where they begin to focus on a certain area of academics and take more courses in that field. So if a certain student decides that they wish to major in biology, does their entire course load consist of nothing but biology classes?

No! Most colleges and universities embrace the liberal arts model. They understand that regardless of a student's desire to major in one particular field, it's vitally important to receive a well-rounded education—one that includes classic literature, foreign languages, history, math, economics, science, as well as unrelated electives that just look interesting. Yes, the student will eventually accrue more credits in biology in order to fulfill the prerequisites of graduating within that major, but along the way they will be required to take subjects that they may not initially be interested in.

There are many reasons why the liberal arts model is such a desirable way to educate students. Kids are taught to think and to solve problems. They are exposed to concepts and ideas that are outside of their comfort zone and realize that the world is bigger than they thought. They become proficient in the language of civilization. And on a more practical level, they will find it easier to get a job. Potential employers love to see applicants with a great liberal arts education. They know that those kids know how to think, solve problems, and to learn on the job.

Most importantly, students at that age might go into one field but over the course of a lifetime would likely move from one job to another. Who can even envision what jobs or fields might exist ten, twenty, or more years in the future? Students need to be educated not for one particular position, but for the ability to adapt to any number of possibilities. Put another way, they need to have the flexibility to make a variety of career choices over the course of a lifetime. Going back to our unfortunate example of students being taught nothing but math for most of their years of education, we realize they would be hopelessly unprepared for much of anything else.

Why can't we take this same worldview and apply it to the vitally important subject of Judaism? We are currently teaching our young kids and b'nei mitzvah students the equivalent of nothing but math for most of their education. And even worse, we're giving them their degree at age thirteen and telling them they've graduated.

So here's one striking one way to reimagine our entire model of b'nei mitzvah training: Let's base our students' Jewish education on the liberal arts model. Just as they will eventually do in the near future, students will learn a certain amount about various areas of Judaism, but will ultimately choose one preferred discipline to zero in on.

This might be implemented in a variety of ways, but taken to its full potential, would mark a complete and utter transformation in how all kids become bar and bat mitzvah. Let's start with more modest changes and progress from there. I believe that all synagogues, kids, and families should be able to integrate these changes to varying degrees. The act of reimagining does not need to consist of tearing everything down and razing all that is familiar (although that's possible too). Instead, some congregations can integrate this material little by little and adapt it to fit their students more appropriately.

Other families—especially those who choose not to affiliate with a congregation—would have more flexibility to create whatever structure they desired.

## The Subjects

If we're looking to the model of a liberal arts education as our ideal, then how does that translate into a Jewish education? What are the various fields that exist within Judaism that we would like our kids to learn?

Here's where we first begin to veer off our well-traveled path of b'nei mitzvah training. Our changes can be substantial and extensive, or could merely represent a slight deviation from what is considered usual. No matter how one chooses to proceed, understand this important fact: Each minute spent studying an alternative area, subject, prayer, field, or domain is likely one fewer minute spent in conventional b'nei mitzvah training. The idea is that every single child does not necessarily need to learn the same set of prayers, melodies, Torah, and haftarah readings. Some may learn less of those and spend more effort on another area. These are the first tentative steps away from the set of what is automatically expected.

So the best way to start reimagining would be to try to identify as many different subjects or areas of interest for a young Jewish person, whether that would be the usual age of thirteen or perhaps at a later time. Put another way, let's create a small-scale Jewish University. What departments would be included in the catalog?

Here are some ideas—and the beauty of this exercise is that this is not an exhaustive list. It's merely one set of suggestions that can always be expanded upon. For now, let's seed our Jewish University catalog with the following academic headings along with their descriptions. Do you have more that I haven't listed? Great—that's exactly the right idea—now I have you reimagining along with me.

### Liturgy and Prayers/Synagogue Skills

This might represent the closest category to the current status quo. For those families who are most comfortable within the synagogue environment and are at home in the sanctuary and within the pages of the siddur, this is a natural place to end up. It also makes a tremendous amount of sense because it is this group of young people who are most likely to use these learned skills repeatedly in the future, whether at a service in the near future, at a Jewish summer camp, at college, or as adults in their own congregations. In this case, the current model of bar or bat mitzvah training will be most relevant and a true entrée into adult Jewish life.

If a student is more musically talented and has a nice singing voice, that kid would be more likely to appreciate and form a basic understanding of the music of the service. What are the different scales that we use for Shabbat morning versus other days of the Jewish calendar? Do they have a favorite tune that could be incorporated into certain parts of the service? If the synagogue is one that utilizes musical instruments on Shabbat, could the student actually play one of those songs while everyone else sang the words? It all depends on the specific case, but each of those examples still involves a level of study and preparation.

## Jewish Sacred Music

Are there any future cantors out there? This field of study would serve as an age-appropriate introduction into not only *how* someone leads a service, but *why* they do it that way. Rather than simply learn and memorize the melody for a set of words in the siddur, kids and teens can start to understand that there are distinct musical modes and scales that are used depending on the occasion (most commonly Shabbat, but also Jewish holidays, weekdays, the new month, and other times during the year). A lot of students play instruments and learn to read music at a young age, and many would be capable of at least a basic understanding of this material.

Included within this department is a detailed look at trope, more than the superficial treatment most kids usually get. The trope symbols represent an incredible musical, literary, and grammatical achievement that was accomplished and recorded by scholars who only had a basic and sometimes ambiguous text to work with. In many cases, the tropes tell us how to interpret the text and can actually change the very meaning of the words. The tropes also served as a primitive but effective public address system in a world without technology—the first trope melodies probably imitated the natural rise and fall of the human voice while a person was speaking and trying to be heard clearly in a large crowd. Most interestingly, the complete set of music and melodies of the tropes came much later.

Going a little further, a lot of students end up learning one way to sing tropes for the haftarah, and then another way to chant the Torah reading (or they simply memorize the two from recordings). In addition to those two sets of melodies, there are four more ways that tropes are sung: reading Torah on the High Holidays; Megillat Esther on Purim; the Book of Lamentations (*Eichah*) on Tisha B'av; and the three different books that are read on each of the three festivals. Some of these trope melodies actually represent the oldest Jewish music in existence.

Not only would some students find this subject fascinating, but it, too, would be exceptionally useful in future years. All of these trope melodies are used throughout the Jewish calendar, and an individual who is proficient in some or all of them would be called upon to take part in services over and over again.

## Jewish Secular Music

There is a huge body of Jewish music that has no direct connection to the synagogue, but is nevertheless a field that could be of enormous interest. In fact, the attraction of this field is that it may be as broadly or narrowly defined as one would like—there is no single, accepted way that one defines what constitutes "Jewish music." One could make the case that any song or composition created by a Jewish person might fall in this category, and Jewish composers or musical performers, whether classical or modern, are too numerous to list. A lot of what we think we know about Jewish music comes from the often unimaginative and at times insipid playlist on the "Jewish Channel" on satellite radio around Chanukah. Wouldn't it be amazing to have young people realize that there's more to Jewish music than "If I Were a Rich Man" and Adam Sandler's "Chanukah Song"?

This can also spark an additional interest in and connection to Israel and that country's list of famous and historic performers and folk musicians.

## Jewish History

This field is purposely vague. Certainly Jewish history could entail any number of different areas. Yes, some students do get a very basic exposure to some aspects of Jewish history as part of Religious School—but I fear that much of that falls in the They-Tried-to-Kill-Us-We-Won-Let's-Eat category. Other possible ideas might be a closer look at how Jewish people came to this country and how the Reform and Conservative Movements got started, Jews in the military (in this or other countries), or specific Jewish historical figures. I know a lot of teachers and Jewish professionals who love exposing kids to Famous Jewish Sports Heroes, which is great, but there's a lot more that different kids would find interesting.

As far as I'm concerned, "history" may refer to anything that's happened in the past—even last week. While some people might find the Jewish presence in the Middle Ages fascinating, I would wager that it's not a natural destination for the average preteen. But a student could examine more recent Jewish events over the course of recent years or months and see how that relates to what and how they learn in school. That would effectively create a lasting and age-appropriate Jewish connection.

## The Holocaust

I listed this subject separately from the more general area of Jewish history. The topic of Holocaust education fills entire volumes. To be sure, there are strong emotions connected with this subject; we are still able to speak with survivors and have access to their firsthand accounts. Some kids do incorporate some aspect of Holocaust education in their b'nei mitzvah ceremonies—sometimes by "twinning" with a child their age who perished during that time and as a result never had the opportunity to celebrate at their own service. Other parents and educators might be of the opinion that certain children are simply not emotionally mature enough to grasp the basic concepts of the Shoah, or feel that it's a subject that they would like to introduce in the home where they have more control over the content.

But for those kids—and that might include those well over the age of thirteen—who are able to connect to this subject on a more mature level, this would obviously make an appropriate focus.

## Jewish Texts

This area of study is also purposely vague. While a lot of us don't necessarily picture the majority of suburban Jewish kids lining up for Talmud study (although some might!), the category of Jewish texts encompasses so many possibilities. The easiest and most familiar set of texts are right in the siddur that many of us use each week—the Shabbat liturgy. This presents a wonderful opportunity for in-depth study and examination of prayers that are already being taught to kids.

They could spend more time delving into particular prayers and really learning what the text means. For instance, one of the better-known prayers in the siddur is the *Ashrei*—mostly consisting of Psalm 145. Many b'nei mitzvah kids learn the usual melody throughout Religious School and eventually master the fairly complicated words. Even years later, I think a lot of these now older teens and young adults can recite at least the opening line of *Ashrei* by memory.

But do they know what any of it means? Do they realize that the text is taken right from the Tanach? Do they realize the beauty of each line's structure—that each line consists of the same idea stated two parallel ways and separated by a comma? Have they noticed that the lines of text are presented in Hebrew alphabetical order? Can they view this text as glorious poetry and appreciate what the original author was trying to accomplish?

Why are some texts written in the first person, while others are written in the second or third person? Why are some singular while others are plural? Which prayers read like poetry while others read like prose? What prayers contain ideas and thoughts that we in modern times would have trouble agreeing with or relating to?

Students could also use what they learn and compose their own set of prayers—and placing those original prayers within the parts of the siddur that make the most sense. This is a project that would be appropriate for b'nei mitzvah students of all ages—their original prayers would reflect where they are at any given stage.

## Israel

Religious School students do likely spend a lot of classroom time devoted to learning about and developing a connection to Israel. Some kids, though, might benefit from going beyond that and really delving into various aspects of our homeland—its history, politics, conflicts, economics, geography. There are countless subjects that one could study. Remember that "forming a connection to Israel" was a likely goal for our b'nei mitzvah families; here's a wonderful opportunity.

Yes, this is already high on the list of priorities even when working within the status quo. But as the rest of b'nei mitzvah preparation, it doesn't necessarily prepare kids to be Jewish adults, knowledgeable and conversant about Israel. Rather, it instills kids with a juvenile-level education. When our kids go on to college and beyond, are they Jewish adults, able to have a cogent dialogue with those who would voice anti-Israel sentiments, or are they still walking around with a thirteen-year-old level of Jewish education?

One popular model for b'nei mitzvah is having the ceremony in Israel—again, this is a wonderful and worthy way to mark this passage. However, in many cases, families are taking the current imperfect model and simply transplanting it in Israel. They contract with a rabbi in Israel who specializes in these ceremonies, and learn a set of prayers and probably a Torah reading that the rabbi provides them. Other than the visceral and powerful experience of actually being at the Wall, on Masada, or wherever the ceremony may take place, there is likely the same lack of actual learning taking place. The student is probably still memorizing everything by rote.

## Jewish Literature

Just as Jewish music may be divided up into separate categories of sacred and secular, so too can we look at the body of Jewish literature. Obviously, the sacred texts, as noted above, might include Talmud, Mishnah, and Tanach, for instance. But then there are countless Jewish authors, both historic and modern, that some students would like to pursue in greater depth. In fact, one valuable question for anyone to ask is this: What makes something *Jewish* literature? Is it anything written by a Jewish author, or must it contain Jewish themes of some kind?

Certainly, there's a wide variety of choices here, and much of it would depend on the student's age.

## Creative Writing/Composing

Let's take the previous fields of study one step further. A lot of teens possess an enormous talent for creativity. In a lot of ways, therefore, the traditional model of b'nei mitzvah training is the exact opposite of what they best connect to. There's little room for anything original or reflective of their own unique personality. The words they recite and the melodies that they chant are those of other people.

What if, instead of memorizing texts to which they have no connection, students were able to create their own? Just as I suggested within the subject of Jewish texts, kids could compose their own set of prayers, built on a foundation and understanding of the existing service. Talented kids could compose their own songs or other melodies used in a service, utilizing the traditional *nusach* (set of modes and scales).

Others may wish to follow their creativity outside the bounds of Jewish worship, composing their own Jewish music (with a rationale for why it's Jewish), or writing a Jewish story or significant project.

## Genealogy/Family History

What's in a name? The appeal of this area of focus is that it encompasses a number of other subjects as well. A b'nei mitzvah student might simply start with his Hebrew name and go on from there:

- What does that name mean? Is it a biblical name? How is that biblical character portrayed in the text? What does the character do or what are they known for?
- Which country or area of the world did the family originally come from?
- Are there still any relatives that are living in that region of the world?
- How was that branch of the family affected by the Holocaust?
- Did relatives pass through Ellis Island or another port of entry? Did they come with their family or make the passage on their own?

Additionally, the increased popularity and easy access to consumer DNA testing kits such as 23andMe make it extremely easy to trace one's genetic heritage. Yes, I imagine that most of the readership of this book would likely see results that read 90+ percent Ashkenazic Jewish, but these products also connect you with probable relatives. It has become fairly easy to discover and make contact with other branches of one's family. Where did they end up? What's their connection to Judaism? Is there a particular characteristic or talent that seems to be a family trait?

Once you get started down this road, there are countless paths to follow.

### Community Service

Like the heading of Liturgy and Synagogue Skills, one could say that Community Service is already built into the existing routine of most kids' b'nei mitzvah. Many synagogues require that all of their students choose some kind of *tzedakah* project or area of community service that benefits a particular cause or organization. A frequent benchmark is for the student to have recorded at least thirteen hours of service, as a symbol of their commitment to Jewish involvement upon reaching the age of b'nei mitzvah. This is a worthy start. But it's also often treated as an afterthought—some additional requirement put in place by the temple in order to "graduate."

Instead, some families and b'nei mitzvah kids might want to make the Community Service aspect the main focus of becoming bar or bat mitzvah. What a superb opportunity to demonstrate that someone is ready to become more involved, more engaged, and more responsible for the world around them.

## Family Education

This is really turning the model of b'nei mitzvah preparation on its head. In fact, it seemingly contradicts something that I wrote back in chapter 6—that having parents in the room during lessons in often counterproductive.

Instead, what if we completely embraced the notion of group learning—specifically that members of the family learn at the same time. Together they decide on an area to pursue, with each person exploring information independently but then coming together to share what they've learned. I imagine that this might prove to be most effective with those families who have kids who are closer in age. This would be the very antithesis of what routinely takes place: the parent pulls up to the curb, drops the kid off, comes back later to watch him come out of the temple, and then spends seven days until the next lesson asking, "Did you practice?"

## Making It All Come Together

You've just paged through some sample pages from our Jewish University minicatalog. Unlike the printed or online course catalogs that are published by actual universities, this one is fluid, changeable, flexible, and very much a work in progress. It's less of a listing of specific areas of study and more of a glimpse into what's possible if families and synagogues felt free to step away from the sanctuary-centric model that all but defines b'nei mitzvah preparation. Chapter 12 will take a more detailed look at how one might implement a course of b'nei mitzvah study, but first let's head right into the eye of the storm. Making a substantial change like this is fraught with difficulty and resistance.

# CHAPTER ELEVEN

~

# The Pushback

*See one. Do one. Teach one.*

If you have any background in the medical field, or if you like to watch TV shows about doctors, you know exactly what this means. It refers to the traditional educational method used to teach students various medical or surgical procedures. Most cynically, it makes a statement about some areas of medical training—that there are certain tasks that are best learned and memorized quickly and then immediately passed on to others. As time goes on, one supposes (and hopes), a person gets much more skilled in these particular areas. But in the meantime, what's the point in spending a lot of time? Here's how to insert an IV. There's no need in going into minute detail on the history of intravenous medication or the development of the equipment used.

The state of b'nei mitzvah training can be compared to this model as well. The emphasis is on a superficial memorizing of a specific item—a prayer, a Torah reading, a haftarah—by seeing or hearing it and then immediately rattling it off. If a student repeats that process enough time ("practice at home for thirty minutes every day") then they will have mastered it. Just as in our example above, there's no pressing need to delve more deeply into any text. No one is prompted to ask *why* is this prayer chanted here? What do these words mean? And if for some reason a student does ask those questions, they're answered quickly so they don't run out of valuable lesson time. Finally, in some congregations or schools, talented and accomplished kids assist in tutoring the younger or more struggling students.

See one. Do one. Teach one.

Since I have no complaints about any medical care I've received in my lifetime, I can assume that all medical training institutions know what they're doing and they have it under control. But we can do a lot better with our kids' Jewish education and the beginning of what we hope is a lifelong connection to Judaism.

From the moment you began reading the first page of this book, you likely had the following reaction: Interesting idea, but it'll never fly. In fact, I have received similar feedback from a number of professional colleagues as I've articulated my vision of reimagining how we prepare kids for b'nei mitzvah. The following typical response came from one colleague after discussing in detail my vision for change: "I LOVE your ideas! [slight pause] I disagree with them, but I love them."

What followed was a point-by-point, robust conversation about how b'nei mitzvah kids learn, what's important to them and their families, and what these kids would likely take away from their experience in both the short- and long-term future. It turned out that my colleague didn't disagree much at all with the ideas I was putting forth. It was a visceral, natural, and predictable resistance to the idea of changing a model that's been in place for as long as anyone can remember. And again, because the status quo works wonderfully for a certain fraction of the Jewish population, it provides just enough of an illusion that it's adequate for everyone.

We've all shared the common experiences that I've described over the preceding chapters. We're all aware that so much of the b'nei mitzvah ceremony is a rote recitation of memorized skills. And we also know that one of most significant challenges is engaging with our students *after* the bar or bat mitzvah and giving their families and them a rationale for maintaining the same level of involvement and connection.

So yes, they understand. But then the opposition begins—because what we do and how we do it is a familiar and accepted part of our routine. As *you* continued reading, your position also became more entrenched as you probably came up with more reasons why there would be little interest or impetus to change something that's been going along fairly successfully or at least without much controversy for generations. It's hard to feel a real motivation to change anything when a student is learning the same material—and in the same way—as their father, grandfather, and great-grandfather did before him. That's a lot of built-in tradition and resistance from every family. And why bother rocking the boat when it's seemingly been working all these years?

Here's why: let's imagine a group of random Jews-on-the-street and get the answer to the question: "What do you remember from your bar or bat mitzvah?"

- I was really nervous.
- My mother got mad at my aunt because she was late to the service.
- Everyone threw candy at me when I finished.
- I skipped a page once and started singing the wrong prayer.
- I was deathly afraid of dropping the Torah.
- I kept watching the cantor to see when he would bow so I would know when to.
- All my friends from school came to my party.
- My parents told me I went way too fast reading my speech.

Perhaps that's human nature: we just remember what we were most nervous about or specific missteps that stick in our mind. Maybe we should ask the question in a better way: "What part of the haftarah, Torah reading, or any page in the service do you remember?"

- I can sing the first three words of my haftarah.
- I know how to sing "amen" when starting a Torah reading.
- I know how to lead the Shema.
- I think I remember the name of my Torah portion.

So when I ask, is it worth rocking the boat when it's been working all these years, my question is: *Is* it really working? If you could fast-forward into the future and ask your adult child or grandchild what they most remember about their b'nei mitzvah experience, I expect that you'd be hoping for better answers than these.

You can make that happen.

## Facing the Tough Questions

I do get it. Change is hard—even the suggestion of change can seem insurmountable. Let's take as many possible arguments against changing the status quo as we can think of and see how we can effect some real change. And above all, remember that this must not be a total and utter transformation of everything that we know. Consider this as a first step in a house renovation. One could repaint the walls and buy a few pieces of furniture, take it to the next level and remodel a bathroom or kitchen, or tear down the existing structure and build a brand-new house from the foundation up. Each scenario is possible but will depend on the willingness (yes, and the finances) of each individual. Reimagining how our kids learn can work the same way—each family or congregation can begin with modest changes or dramatically alter the entire Jewish educational landscape.

Let's address the pushback.

**Myth**: B'nei mitzvah ceremonies must include reading a haftarah or chanting from the Torah.

**Fact**: Remember back to what I told you in chapter 1. Children do not turn into bar or bat mitzvah kids when they read Torah or chant (by rote) a haftarah. Rather, they do those things to publicly demonstrate that they are ritually able to. Traditionally, the bar mitzvah ceremony was a commemoration of the fact that a child had reached the magic (and arbitrary) age of thirteen and could therefore take part in leading and participating in a service as any fellow Jewish adult.

So what would happen if a child did not prepare a Torah reading, learn to chant a haftarah, or lead a service? Nothing at all—there is no magic transformation that occurs after the completion of the service. Just as there is a qualifying age for various activities—voting, drinking, serving in the military to name a few—so too is there the moment when a child can take part in and be counted as part of a Jewish service. That takes place regardless of any training or ceremony.

A child may prepare (or for that matter, not prepare) to become bar or bat mitzvah at any age and in any manner. It has no bearing whatsoever on that individual's standing within the Jewish community.

**Myth**: Sure, anyone can deviate from the traditional b'nei mitzvah ceremony, but it wouldn't be authentic.

**Fact**: The word "authentic" is a lot like "traditional." In many cases, it refers to the way people remember a certain thing has always been done. People tend to look at Conservative Judaism for instance, and define it as a way to maintain authenticity within the context of traditional Judaism.

Now think back to the origins of the Conservative Movement. Do you think Rabbi Solomon Schechter stood on the steps of the recently established Jewish Theological Seminary around the turn of the twentieth century and ever envisioned Conservative rabbis officiating at same-sex marriages? Could the Jewish leaders of that time have ever foreseen a time when women would be ordained as rabbis? Would they have deemed either of those milestones as "authentic?" Of course not.

We are in charge of the direction we take as Jews, whether individually, congregationally, or affiliating with a movement. Change, whether dramatic or incremental, will take place when enough people decide that it's needed.

We cantors have a little in-joke: People tend to complain when we introduce new, unfamiliar melodies. "Please, Cantor, can't you just sing the *tradi-*

*tional* melody?" In fact, if I introduce a new tune, and sing it for three weeks in a row, people actually forget that it was once new and begin to think of that as the "traditional" melody. I'm not exaggerating. Three weeks. Bottom line: we can initiate whatever changes that we deem appropriate and they can become accepted, authentic, and traditional.

**Myth**: All b'nei mitzvah ceremonies must take place in a service.

**Fact**: Not only is this one false, I'll go even further. There doesn't even need to be any kind of ceremony at all, whether it involves a service or not. Remember how I explained that a young Jewish person becomes bar or bat mitzvah automatically, simply by reaching the age of majority—set at thirteen according to tradition. Everything else—the service, the preparation, the lessons, the Torah readings, the haftarah, the party, and all the rest of it—only serve to show and acknowledge this crossing of that threshold. But whether there's a ceremony or not, once any Jewish child opens their eyes on the morning after their thirteenth birthday according to the Jewish calendar, they are eligible to receive and participate in all the same honors and rituals as anyone else.

Recognizing this new status in the context of a service does involve a certain amount of logic. Many of the rituals that are now available, such as being counted toward a minyan, receiving an aliyah, or being allowed to lead the service, take place in the sanctuary. So if the b'nei mitzvah ceremony evolved as a result of being able to showcase a person's new status to perform these rituals, it made a lot of sense for that to occur during services.

That still provides a compelling reason to combine the b'nei mitzvah rite of passage with a service. But in some cases, it doesn't need to be the sole focus—or even included at all. A new way of thinking says that there are multiple and varied ways that a Jewish teen can form and recognize a new connection to Judaism on an adult level—whether that's through increased activism, deeds of charity and fundraising, the pursuit of knowledge in Jewish history or music, an experience in Israel, or any number of non-worship experiences.

The supposedly sacrosanct requirement that all students must perform at a service provides a formidable barrier to many families that for one reason or another—financial, spiritual, geographical—are not able or willing to affiliate with a synagogue. Instead, when we reimagine how and what our kids learn, we are able to create new pathways for families. All of a sudden, this becomes a process of inclusion rather than existing within the narrow domain of ritual performance with which only some Jews are comfortable.

**Myth**: This sounds like a major dumbing down of what has taken place for generations.

**Fact**: This is the "grumpy old man" of myths. Can't you picture him? There he is, sitting in his ancient rocking chair bemoaning the state of "kids today." He says, "When I was a kid, we didn't have [fill in the blank]. We had to get right home from school, get to work on our chores, and then get our homework done." Eventually, you'll also hear about teachers being strict and not allowing any form of misbehavior or you'd suffer the unbearable and likely painful consequences of an angry parent.

Now ask him about his memories of having a bar mitzvah.

"Back in my day, we had to learn the whole Torah reading. The rabbi was an old, nasty Jewish man who drilled us over and over and would snap at us if we made the slightest mistake." He might continue by recalling coming home crying to his parents that he hated the whole thing but they ignored his complaints and made him practice the readings over and over before he was allowed to go out and play. On the day of his bar mitzvah, his voice cracked with nervousness as he made his way through the meaningless words in front of his ancient aunts, uncles, and other relatives. (Okay, he might have pleasant memories of being allowed to drink a schnapps with the older men after services.)

What, then, is his compelling reason to make today's generation prepare for b'nei mitzvah the same way? Simply because that's what he had to do, and he managed to get through it. Never mind that most of his memories of his bar mitzvah are negative, he doesn't retain any material from that time, and the learning itself was miserable. You just have to get through it because that's the way it's done.

If I can return to my comparison to medical training (no, I'm not a secretly frustrated doctor), the we-did-it-that-way-in-my-day came up recently within that field. We all remember reading or hearing about medical residents who had to work thirty-six-hour shifts. They'd get a day or two off and then go back on for another thirty-six hours at a time. Eventually people came to the not-so-surprising conclusion that the fatigued residents who were nearing the end of these marathon shifts were more apt to make major errors and endanger the lives of their patients. As a result, many training hospitals restructured their residents' shifts. They received the same training hours but spread out in a more sensible way to maximize health and safety.

That sounds pretty sensible, but there was pushback. "The thirty-six-hour shift model has been a staple of medical education for as long as we can remember," said many older and established doctors. It's a rite of passage and is intended to train new doctors to operate effectively under stress and fatigue. In other words—the same argument against that change is the same argument here. We all did it that way and came out fine. Why are we always looking to make things easy for the next generation?

But this vision of reimagining is *not* dumbing anything down. On the contrary, it represents an elevation of the process, recognizing that kids have amazing abilities and a wide variety of interests. We seek to view kids and families as individuals, not a vague mass of congregants who must all walk the exact same path. In fact, it's our grumpy old man who was provided with a dumbed-down experience—it consisted of memorization and busywork that had no utility in later years.

**Myth**: This will be a major blow to the strength of synagogue life. Without being able to depend on the familiar path of kids becoming b'nei mitzvah in the sanctuary at age thirteen, many congregations will lose countless members, and their existence will be in jeopardy.

**Fact**: Another myth that we can file in the "people hate change" category. Under the typical synagogue model, most of the income depends on young families with young children who (rightly) seek to connect with the local Jewish community and enroll their kids in the Religious School—paying both dues and tuition for all the years leading up to that one, highly anticipated event: the bar or bat mitzvah. Much like older parents who can't wait to make that very last college tuition payment, the bar or bat mitzvah date is seen as the culmination of all those years of financial obligation, endless carpools, and constant complaining from kids who had already sat for hours in school and didn't relish the thought of another few hours in a synagogue classroom.

So yes, the synagogue does depend on this particular process and demographic for its financial stability.

But let's go further: Why is it this particular group that is most present and ready to commit resources to the synagogue? One might think that older families, perhaps empty nesters who are at the top of their professional lives and are nearing retirement, would be a more likely source of financial support. Often, however, these families have already left the temple, expressing sincere regret after years of membership, with statements such as these: "We just don't use the temple anymore," or "We just can't justify spending a few thousand dollars." This is a sad consequence of our b'nei mitzvah culture. When most synagogue life revolves around the perpetuation of the b'nei mitzvah factory, there are few resources left for any other age group.

Students disappear after the magic age of thirteen.

Once ever-present families now stop coming to services because there are more pressing demands on their time.

Older members have little to connect them with the congregation that is focused so much on young families.

Because generations of Jews have gone through the b'nei mitzvah process in the same way, we're now seeing the consequences. When services, Torah reading, and haftarah are the only skills taught to Jewish kids who are then told "You're a man now!", why are we surprised when later in life they realize there's nothing compelling to connect them to a synagogue?

By changing and, yes, disrupting now, we're investing in the vibrancy and survival of Jewish congregations later. No one has been playing the long game. Everything has been viewed in the short term: getting a kid to thirteen and doing what is needed to stage an impressive performance. As for what happens after that—we just hope for the best.

If synagogues instead strived to meet all students where they are—allowing them to thrive and revel in their unique abilities and recognizing that not everyone wants or needs to lead a service—think how that will be remembered and internalized by current and future generations.

**Myth:** The set age of thirteen provides a necessary structure and time line for Jewish education and families' commitment. If you take away any mandated age, many families will simply put it off until it's more convenient—a time that will likely never come.

**Fact:** There's some merit to this argument. But I think the risk of some families simply never pursuing having any bar or bat mitzvah at all can be minimized.

First, remember that there's no requirement to have a b'nei mitzvah ceremony. So even if a family does put it off to some indeterminate time in the future, this doesn't affect anyone's Jewish status. There's no such thing as a kid who was never "bar mitzvahed" or "bat mitzvahed."

Second, our whole premise is that there's little reward in having a bar or bat mitzvah ceremony for no other reason than thinking that it just has to be done. Those families who actively attend services—whose kids love to be a part of the rituals and look forward to one day taking a more active role—will be perfectly happy and well served with the status quo. But we can all imagine families that join a synagogue so their kids will have a bar or bat mitzvah, after which they have no further need for a congregation and resign their membership.

If kids are presented early on with the possibility of learning what's important to them, they will be more motivated to learn and have their status in the Jewish community recognized.

**Myth:** Kids will rise to the occasion when they have a significant level of expectation placed upon them.

**Fact:** No myth here; I couldn't agree more. However, it's not the level of expectation that kids can and should respond to, but rather the quality of that expectation.

Yes, most kids who progress through the usual routine of b'nei mitzvah lessons do end up mastering (i.e., memorizing) the material fairly well. They begin with the usual feeling of being overwhelmed at the vast quantity of *stuff* that they'll have to learn and ultimately sing in public. As each week goes by and the lessons proceed, they do chip away at the mountain of prayers, texts, and melodies. Finally, they are able to look back and feel a sense of accomplishment and pride at having faced up to a formidable task and tackled it. That feeling of pride is indeed a wonderful goal that we should be aiming for in any model of the b'nei mitzvah ritual. It's a true life skill—one that any young person would hopefully look back on repeatedly whenever faced with more challenges.

But we are still assigning skills that are not themselves useful in many cases. When we respect kids enough to meet them where they are, acknowledge their current position on faith and community, inquire as to what *they* find most compelling about Judaism rather than what *we* think—then you will see each student not only rise to meet our expectations, but soar past that level and exceed them.

**Myth:** Early Jewish education and training for b'nei mitzvah is all about "planting seeds" for the future. It provides a positive and tangible experience that we're betting will pay off in a myriad of ways as the individual eventually becomes an (actual) adult and has a family of their own.

**Fact:** Sure, I'll go with that to a certain extent. But you can't identify the sole, overarching goal of becoming b'nei mitzvah as trying to distill a certain experience that you hope will blossom later. Instead, b'nei mitzvah education should be about learning actual material that is relevant to the individual and their family right now. In addition to our lofty future aspirations, there has to be some practical and tangible learning and application to a student's life—today. It should entail making a connection to Judaism in a way that means something. It makes little sense to spend months drilling service skills with a kid whose family is unlikely to ever regularly attend services, with the vague and general hope that one day, in some imaginary time, this kid will decide to enter a synagogue and will feel instantly at home because they memorized some prayers.

We don't make kids who hate sports try out for the football team.

We don't make kids who can't hold pitch join the choir.

We don't make kids who can only draw stick figures enroll in advanced art class.

But we currently take *every* kid and attempt to teach them a host of synagogue skills, without any apparent regard for their skills or interests. We're not meeting these kids where they are. Rather, we're remaining immovable and insisting that they come to us.

In the previous couple of chapters, I've laid out some alternate areas of study that many Jewish adults and professionals would certainly agree are relevant and vital for any Jewish adult to learn. And I then identified many of the supposed reasons why none of that will work—and together we saw that much of that resistance is a result of our inertia or significant misunderstanding of what becoming b'nei mitzvah actually means. Now let's turn to the next chapter and see how we might put this into practice.

~

# CHAPTER TWELVE

# The Vision

Have you ever received this proposal from your local car dealership: "You can drive a brand-new car and still keep your current car payment!"

One reason why such a sales pitch is so attractive is that it builds upon the appeal of the status quo. You can make a substantial improvement, but without having to endure any change. So let me start with such an offer: we can institute many changes in how we prepare kids to become b'nei mitzvah while retaining the current structure and time commitment of lessons. In other words, you can have an entirely new b'nei mitzvah experience and still keep your current Jewish infrastructure. The same Jewish professionals or tutors who teach our kids how to chant *mercha tipcha* would also be qualified to oversee some of these changes.

Again, there are no one-size-fits-all solutions here. All of my suggested changes—including courses of study and varied timetables—are just that: suggestions. They're options. If I told you that all b'nei mitzvah families must embrace certain specific changes in order to make the ceremony relevant and modern, then I would be doing as much a disservice to you as those who say that we shouldn't change anything. One size does not fit all. Everything I am presenting represents various options on a menu.

Using the model of a Jewish University that we talked about in chapter 10, let's examine two possible ways of approaching the material. These are merely sample templates and, by design, are purposely vague.

## The Horizontal Model

This first model will more closely resemble how most families and Jewish professionals already prepare b'nei mitzvah students. I'm calling it "horizontal" because it moves laterally—beginning a set number of months before a planned date and progressing consistently throughout that time. Picture a very long table: we begin the material all the way on one end and gradually make our way over to the other end—the bar or bat mitzvah date.

Building upon the liberal arts model, the early lessons might consist of general discussions on various subjects, with the goal of determining those areas that appeal the most to the student. As much as I discouraged a parental presence during lessons back in chapter 6, I recognize that this approach would make an ideal venue for parents and teen to sit, learn, and discuss together. The difference is that these would be informative sessions, filled with exploration, discussions, and an eye toward discovering sparks of passion. This is in contrast to the usual first few lessons, which mainly consist of this: "Here's your haftorah. Now let's start learning trope."

In such a model, I would encourage parents to share their own experiences, adding depth to their child's future learning. For instance, if we start talking about Jewish literature, it would be wonderful to hear a parent recount a book from their own past that caused them to think about being Jewish in a new light. If we had a session on Jewish history, we might trace what the parents learned about the Jewish people versus what students today tend to focus on. Consider these first sessions (notice that I am not calling them "lessons") as the core curriculum of our liberal arts school. They should cover a lot of disparate areas in a general way, and therefore would take a good bit of time. Included in this introductory material would also be the traditional areas of trope and prayers. So looking again at our table metaphor, we are still sitting all the way to one end; we haven't really started moving much yet.

As we progress a little bit, either with or without the involvement of parents, we can start thinking about focusing in a little. Put another way, it might be time to pick a major. What is the student most passionate about or interested in? What matches most with the life they are living now? What would keep them wanting to come back each week? Finally, what would enhance the Jewish life that they and their family are living right now?

We're now moving horizontally along the table a little bit. Our sessions or lessons (the actual material we're learning helps us decide which word to use) are now spent mostly on one subject or domain. The teacher—whether it's the cantor, rabbi, or other hired tutor—acts more like a coach or advisor rather than presenting a wall of material. I envision this much like a traditional model of Jewish learning called *chavruta* style—in which two or more participants act like equal partners, examining material together and engaging in discussion. Each gains value from being exposed to the other's point of view and how they understand the text or problem. Being free to explore ideas with an engaged student like that would be a dream come true for most teachers.

One possible version of this approach has the student concurrently learning (or memorizing) the more traditional material, such as trope or certain prayers. Part of the decision making that goes into this method determines whether the family would like to make a service the primary focus of this process or more peripheral to the learning.

The culmination of this learning could be presented in a variety of ways. A more traditional approach would be to have a service, with the bar or bat mitzvah student leading or chanting whatever amount they had learned. But alongside this conventional presentation of skills, they could present a summarized version of what they had learned or researched, what it meant to then, and how they connected with it—and this could be part of an extended speech or presentation or a creative display suitable for the synagogue lobby or celebration. The main point is to highlight the individual's effort and the connection of each person. Therefore, there shouldn't be just one way of doing it. Wouldn't it be fascinating to walk into a bar or bat mitzvah service in temple each week and have no idea at all what to expect?

## The Timetable

Like every other aspect of our reimagined b'nei mitzvah preparation, there's not one acceptable timetable. If kids are engaged, interested, and invested in what they're learning, they can get a lot accomplished over a certain amount of time.

But taken generally, this type of model could work very well using the existing framework already in use in many synagogues. Most kids begin their lessons six, nine, or even twelve months ahead of time; any of those blocks of time could work, with the student and teacher meeting once a week. And extending our vision of the liberal arts method, the more general and varied material would be discussed early on in the process. Only later would it make more sense to specialize in one area.

Another consideration is each student's particular schedule. As noted in an earlier chapter, kids often have an enormously complicated schedule. I'm purposely not using the cliché "overprogrammed," because I don't necessarily believe that it's a negative. On the contrary, I love the fact that kids have access to so many worthwhile activities. If you think about it—they're taking this liberal arts model and applying it to their own lives. They have the opportunity to try out and be active in many varied activities—sports, music, dance, drama, and so on—and in the process hope to find their passion.

This is often the moment when our kids become alienated from Jewish life. We insist that for this one year, they need to drop everything. B'nei mitzvah lessons must become the one and only priority. Play rehearsals? Sorry, you can't be in that production. Soccer games? You'll have to give up your place on the team. We're coming along and taking the joy of exploration away from young kids at precisely the time when they're developing their own strengths and interests, and we're telling them, "*This* one and only thing is so important you must put every other activity aside" (until the next year, when it won't be important anymore).

Don't misunderstand what I'm saying. I believe strongly that Judaism and our kids' Jewish education and connection are of paramount importance. That's the entire point of this book—that we're falling short on what we should be able to accomplish. So just as the one traditional method of b'nei mitzvah preparation is no longer appropriate in many cases, so too is our usual admonition that all of our kids need to drop everything so they can concentrate solely on learning material for their b'nei mitzvah.

## The Vertical Model

The horizontal model examined b'nei mitzvah preparation in a linear fashion—much like it exists today. Start at point A and finish a certain amount of time later at point B. In many ways, this is a two-dimensional educational model. We stay flat on the table and move from one end to the other.

But what would happen if we added an additional dimension? As soon as we become flexible on time—start dates, age, duration of study, ending date—many more possibilities begin to open up. While this brings us further away from what's considered familiar, it creates a more logical educational experience.

With the vertical model, all options are on the metaphorical table. The specific timing is based on a family's decision on when they feel their child is most able to absorb and appreciate a program designed to form an adult connection to Judaism. For some kids, that works fine at age twelve. Others would do better closer to fifteen or sixteen.

Using the vertical model, we begin learning about various areas of interest—the so-called core curriculum. This might begin at the usual age. But instead of progressing immediately from one thing to the next, we can build

### As an Aside . . .

I've heard a lot of well-meaning statements from parents and colleagues over the years about how kids should demonstrate their commitment to Jewish education. But usually these statements take the form of identifying any other activity as a direct threat to a child's Jewish involvement. They see it as a zero-sum game—one hour spent doing some activity is one fewer hour devoted to Jewish education.

For instance, one parent told me that he simply did not allow his son to participate in any extracurricular activities at all beginning in elementary school through the bar mitzvah year. According to the parent, this would certainly ensure that there would be no conflict with Religious School attendance or any scheduled lesson. I also believe that it would ensure a lifelong resentment of synagogue involvement and attendance.

Some parents are dismissive of what their kids find interesting. I recall one father scoffing at all the kids who have soccer practice after school and occasionally are not able to be present in Hebrew school. His implication was that every parent thought their kid would be a soccer superstar and in the process they were losing what was truly important.

I do feel that a life of Jewish connection is one of the most valuable legacies that we can bequeath to our kids. For the record, I don't believe that soccer practice is more compelling than a Jewish education. But at the same time, giving our kids the opportunity to be well-rounded, to be active within the general community, and to explore what they feel passionate about—those things that are beyond valuable and will make them more complete people and ultimately better Jews.

Just as we can and should tailor b'nei mitzvah training to the individual, why can't we devise a schedule that works for each kid without their having to give up the rest of their lives?

more time into the process, much as universities identify a general course of study for freshmen, but then expect older students—juniors and seniors—to take more advanced and specialized courses in a later year.

Put another way, the horizontal model takes the entire course of educational study and makes it consecutive and continuous. The vertical model more closely resembles an actual program of study, where a student begins at one time and then slowly builds upon previous learning with more advanced and sophisticated material—appearing much as rungs on a (vertical) ladder.

The major benefit to this method, as disruptive as it may seem to the status quo, is that each step along the way may be age-appropriate. A

**As an Aside . . .**

Confirmation is a routine ceremony within the Reform Movement, and I think that it serves as a wonderfully appropriate model for many other Jewish communities. The course leading to Confirmation acknowledges that not only does Jewish learning not end at b'nei mitzvah age—it's actually just getting started. One (admittedly extreme) vision that I have had while writing this book is to simply and completely discontinue the entire bar or bat mitzvah rite of passage. Instead, we co-opt the tradition of Confirmation and make it the one Jewish coming-of-age ceremony for all.

In general, high-school kids are more sophisticated—intellectually, emotionally, and socially—and would have a greater appreciation for all areas of Jewish study. Let middle-school kids be kids and not pretend that they're suddenly mini-adults. If I were on the ancient planning committee to design the perfect time to welcome young Jews into the adult committee, I would vote for age sixteen over all other options.

twelve-year-old will begin with general learning that's appropriate to that age level. Closer to the end of the learning, a fifteen- or sixteen-year-old can handle much deeper and more detailed material. Back in chapter 9, I emphasized how important it is to identify your goals. Other than knowing that this is simply something that you have to get through, what are you really trying to accomplish? Many of us would agree that one common and underlying motivation is to allow young people to establish a nascent connection to Judaism on an adult level. This vertical model goes a long way to help kids do just that.

## The Infrastructure

Reading all of this, you might be reminded of those elaborate toys you desired more than anything for your birthday or for Chanukah—only to bring the heavy box home and see, "Batteries not included. Some assembly required." That was when you knew this wasn't going to be a simple operation. Yes, you'd get to play with the thing eventually, but it would take a while, and probably involve some barely audible parental cursing and maybe a couple of trips to the local store ("I thought it said AA batteries, not AAA").

Luckily, for most of our proposed changes—horizontal, vertical, content, tracks, ceremonies, core curriculum—most synagogues already have the necessary pieces in place. Yes, there might need to be a reshuffling of who does what and when. But massive assembly is not required; this model is pretty much ready to go right out of the box.

Let's imagine we have a typical synagogue where the cantor does much of the tutoring, assisted by either the rabbi (often the closer for the student's D'var Torah) or another hired tutor. During the week, there are a set number of teaching slots, during the afternoon and evenings, when kids come in for their lessons, lasting anywhere from thirty to sixty minutes.

In a traditional, horizontal model, all of the kids will belong to that year's b'nei mitzvah class—typically the seventh grade. Depending on their dates, they will be at varying levels of preparation. Some will have just started recently and might be struggling over each unfamiliar word of the haftarah, while others are nearing the end and can do a respectable job of getting through all the pages. The cantor, rabbi, and/or tutor cover all of the lesson slots.

Now imagine the same general number of kids, and while some are at the usual age of thirteen, some are older—maybe fifteen or sixteen. Some kids are discussing how current events are reminding them of events in Jewish history, while others are showing what they've been able to accomplish with an extensive community service project that they've piloted. Still others might be discussing a book that they read by a Jewish author and how it reminded them of some things that they see at home and in temple. All of these fascinating sessions don't require guest faculty or specially trained individuals who are brought in for this purpose. The existing Jewish professional staff are more than qualified, willing, and able to discuss and teach these topics. To borrow a real estate term, this model is move-in ready.

Furthermore, we can make minor or major changes irrespective of synagogue affiliation to a certain movement or no movement at all. Looking at two of the most common examples of synagogue life—Conservative and Reform Judaism—the model of training is similar in structure. Sure, the actual content and duration of the lessons may vary, but the idea is the same. Show up, meet with the clergy, practice a text or section, come back next week, rinse, repeat. As a result, making any of these changes would work the same way; the existing teaching infrastructure already would make it possible to experiment with different models.

## The Ceremony

Way back in chapter 1, I described what was probably the origin of the bar mitzvah ceremony—that is, it was no ceremony at all. Rather, it was simply a regular, somewhat routine Shabbat morning service. Because there was one young individual who had turned thirteen according to the Jewish calendar, in keeping with Jewish tradition, he was now eligible to take part in the service and participate in certain rituals to a much greater degree than he could just last week. Therefore, the guys who ran the service (and yes, because this is a flashback, all of our players are male), made sure to call him up for an aliyah to the Torah. This was a true cause for celebration for everyone, because it marked an actual and organic progression. It was also assumed correctly that this boy and his father would be present over the following weeks and months.

This service-based b'nei mitzvah ceremony is almost universally the one and only model in use today. We use it to commemorate the b'nei mitzvah of virtually every Jewish person—those who attend synagogue services regularly and those who have barely set foot in a service and are just as unlikely to in the future. So in reimagining how to restructure, or even how to create from scratch, a new, appropriate way to mark a Jewish young person's coming of age, we should take the same approach as we have tried to do with the material learned: we should strive to match the result with the needs and interests of the teen and their family.

Keep in mind, the goal is not to mindlessly and recklessly tear down everything that is familiar. As in the traditional model of learning synagogue skills, prayers, and reading a haftarah, celebrating the moment of becoming b'nei mitzvah works perfectly well for a specific group of people. I might suggest not changing a single thing.

But if many other young teens of varying ages have embarked upon courses of study that represent a multitude of areas of Jewish study, then there's every reason to re-evaluate how that will culminate. It may indeed be within the context of a Shabbat service—and it might also take place in one's home, at a special recognition ceremony during Hebrew school, or at another venue altogether. What is most important is that the ceremony properly reflects the actual learning that took place. It should be the final steps of a long and satisfying journey, rather than a random destination never to be visited again.

However the ceremony is structured, the teen's emotional and intellectual growth needs to be recognized and celebrated. Instead of the usual, "In this week's Torah portion, we read about . . ." (again, fine for some kids), let's hear about a book that a teen read that they will never forget. It would be wonderful to know in detail about a young person's great-grandparents who lived in Eastern Europe and how they emigrated to this country. How amazing would it be to hear a teenager sing an original song using words from the siddur with an explanation of what they mean and why they were chosen?

## But Is It Real?

I thought now would be a good time to unearth that tired and often misunderstood word: *authentic*.

There is the perception that unless there is an actual bar or bat mitzvah service—complete with clergy officiant, Torah, and congregation—then it is *not* a real thing. You can forgive most people for thinking that way given that we've been doing exactly that, unchanged, for generations. I have shared these ideas with fellow clergy—experienced, knowledgeable, and sophisticated colleagues—and their eyes light up with the idea of exploring new traditions. Yet I will still get the question, "But how does he actually get bar mitzvahed?"

So as you read this, remember the most important and overarching fact: That's not a thing. A person cannot get bar or bat mitzvahed. Young Jewish teens are considered b'nei mitzvah the instant they turn thirteen—no different than marking a car's mileage by watching the numbers on the odometer change. We have been talking not about how to effect a change upon a child, but rather how and when that child, with his family, decides how to recognize and celebrate that change. The ceremony should be a natural point along that path. Then it will be among the most authentic moments in their life.

# CHAPTER THIRTEEN

~

# The Paths Forward

The previous chapters have identified three distinct time periods: past, present, and future. For us to effect positive change and expect worthwhile results, it's vital to understand how and why Jewish children have come to prepare for their b'nei mitzvah in a certain way, and why that one model has endured throughout multiple generations, even as Jewish communities themselves have undergone sweeping changes.

What's next? Other than existing as an interesting exercise in Jewish thought, how do we begin to change the way that we think about b'nei mitzvah ceremonies and preparation? This book is all about reimagining. We've done a lot of that. Now, how do we make things truly happen?

There are actually two parallel paths forward—one for families, whether affiliated with a synagogue or not, and one for synagogue professionals themselves. Let's look at how each of these groups can begin to take the first steps along their path.

## Families

Most decisions would naturally begin here. Individual families—and in many cases the parents—decide how they choose to involve themselves in Jewish life. Should we join a synagogue? What type or movement of Judaism best represents our outlook on religious life? How observant do we wish to be? How often will we decide to attend services?

So it would seem completely natural for the path toward the recognition of becoming b'nei mitzvah to be a family decision as well. Instead, in most cases, families cede all control of this process over to the professionals, who they assume know what's best for them and their children.

I propose the following strategies for parents, along with their kids, as they anticipate the time leading up to b'nei mitzvah.

## 1. Ask

What seems to be simple and obvious is often overlooked. As many Jewish families follow what they think is the single path toward their children's b'nei mitzvah, the process surprisingly allows for minimal questioning by anyone involved. If the underlying message from the synagogue and every Jewish professional is, "We know what we're doing and we've been doing this a long time," then by its very nature, posing any kind of probing question is seen as a challenge to others' knowledge and authority. It's ironic that Jewish tradition prides itself on being a religion of questioning and searching for ever more evolving answers to complicated problems, and at the same time we have effectively shut down most feedback in this one vital area.

So . . . ask. And start in the closed circle of your family as you really evaluate what it means to become b'nei mitzvah. Go back and reread chapter 9, where I transition from "Where We Are" to "Where We Can Be." This chapter suggests a beginning strategy of evaluation—not only looking at the whole process but additionally taking an honest look at the individual. Each child and their parents bring different goals and meaning to becoming b'nei mitzvah.

I love the idea of framing these initial questions in the positive. For instance, when beginning the discussion with kids, think about the following ideas:

Instead of "Do you want to have a bar or bat mitzvah?"
**Ask**
"What do you think is the most exciting thing about becoming bar or bat mitzvah?"

Instead of "What is the part that you're most nervous about?"
**Ask**
"What's your biggest strength and makes you feel the most confident?"

Instead of "You're going to have lessons each week. Which activity do you think you can cut back on?"

**Ask**
"What's one thing that you would love to accomplish?

Instead of "Why do we have to do this?!"
**Ask**
"What can we all get out of this journey?"

By posing these introductory questions, you can begin to think about becoming b'nei mitzvah as a logical step—reflecting each child's individual talents and interests—rather than a necessary but secretly dreaded ordeal that each Jewish family has to endure.

## 2. Imagine

That's the whole point of this book, isn't it—reimagining what our kids learn. I love the imagery that goes along with this verb. It implies that anything is possible and that what we can accomplish as a Jewish community and as Jewish individuals has no limit. The only constraints are those that we impose upon ourselves.

Building upon the ideas that I suggested in the previous chapters, think (*imagine!*) what an ideal bar or bat mitzvah ceremony would look like. For now, you don't have to adhere to any rules or imitate past b'nei mitzvah that you have seen or heard about. These ideas, the things that we imagine, are best framed with "Could . . . ?"

- **Could** our ceremony be completely nonreligious?
- **Could** our ceremony take place outside of a synagogue?
- **Could** we wait until our child is a little older and better able to grasp mature concepts?
- **Could** our child learn about various Jewish subjects instead of focusing on leading a service?
- **Could** we find the perfect way to form a lasting connection to being Jewish—something that will be remembered long after the b'nei mitzvah date?
- **Could** we be truly excited about this next stage of our family's Jewish development?

Once you start asking these "could" questions, it actually becomes hard to stop. It's a way to jump-start your thinking and helps to reinforce the idea that change is possible. Undertaking a new way of considering what it means to be b'nei mitzvah is not a rejection of anything. Rather, we're joyfully embracing what may be possible. Imagine what that might feel like.

### 3. Advocate

And here's where I believe the first challenge arises. This is not necessarily an easy step, for a variety of reasons. First, there's the very real issue of peer pressure—upon not only the child, but also upon the parents. No one wants to be the outlier. When your entire peer group (kids or fellow adults) are all traveling one specific path, it would be difficult to be the only family that takes a fork in the road and announces, "We're doing it *this* way instead!"

That's why the act of reimagining works best as a process. You first began by asking any number of open-ended questions about what your family's religious and developmental priorities were. Hopefully you began to understand what sort of learning or time line would be the most appropriate fit for your child. Then with some of these answers in mind, you allowed yourself the opportunity to imagine what that might look like and how it would work. Put another way, those first two steps comprise the simple question, "What if . . . ?"

Here we take the first steps in making it happen. Advocating for something is not synonymous with challenging (although it certainly could be). I believe strongly that Jewish professionals are thrilled with families who are engaged and active throughout the b'nei mitzvah process. I have had families make multiple appointments to sit down and talk about their kids' services or specific personalities, and I always welcome such conversations. The process of advocating does not need to be one-sided—"Here is what I want and I insist that you make it happen." That sort of confrontational attitude isn't good for anyone; it closes you off as much as it shuts out anyone else.

Here are some other ways to effectively *advocate* for what you consider important:

- Have a conversation with your Jewish professionals—but make it a true back-and-forth where each side listens to the other's viewpoints.
- Share your thinking with other parents. My guess is you'll be expressing out loud what they've also been thinking.
- Speak up when something really goes against what you believe. There is no monolithic way that dictates what we must believe, observe, act, or learn within Judaism.

While it's true that others might be more knowledgeable about Jewish traditions and ritual than you, no one knows your child better than you do.

As I've said before, "But we've always done it this way" is not a good reason to submit to a process that you feel, deep down, will not be a true reflection of your values and strengths.

Be open. You can advocate without becoming entrenched in one set position. Hopefully you'll learn of more opportunities to accomplish what you have in mind.

## 4. Adapt

If you approach this entire process as an opportunity to learn and grow, then by definition, you have to make changes and be open to other interpretations and opinions. It's also possible that all of you—parents and child—have made assumptions about what a future bar or bat mitzvah ceremony will look like, and as you proceed, you might realize that something different is taking shape.

Here are some questions that you can consider along the way:

- As you take your first steps along the road to b'nei mitzvah, have you discovered anything new that affects how you imagine the process would unfold?
- How is your child connecting to the material?
- Do you think that this is the right age for this milestone? Is there any value in postponing? What age do you think would be best?

I love the concept of adapting, because it forces the family out of a typically passive position. In most cases, everyone else (temple, professionals, tutors) call the shots. They determine the schedule of lessons and exactly what material will be taught. Parents and kids simply react—by showing up and learning (memorizing) what they're told and how they're directed. But the notion of adaptation means that family members have become active participants in the process. Even if we were to make no changes at all to the current model of b'nei mitzvah preparation, I would urge every family to adapt—that is, to be proactive and visible partners in their kids' learning. Whether we utterly redefine what it means to become b'nei mitzvah or we remain in the existing process, there is ample opportunity for adapting to change.

Don't be afraid to shift positions and decide that something isn't going the way you envisioned.

## 5. Disrupt

I didn't include this item to be provocative, and just as I wrote when telling you to advocate for yourself and your child, the idea is not to be confrontational.

However, no new creative endeavor ever took place without a measure of disruption. And certainly, this entire book represents a disruption—whether very minor or completely paradigm shifting—of how virtually every Jew defines what it means to become b'nei mitzvah and how one learns and prepares for that event. It's okay to disrupt. The Jewish religion itself exists because of Abraham—the very first disrupter and history's first iconoclast.

Our strength and our survival have never been a result of blind obedience to authority. Instead, we are taught that the Jewish way to relate to God, Torah, tradition, and ritual is to question. We have thrived because as the years have unfolded, the Jewish people have evolved and changed as necessary:

- Our ancestors used to bring sacrifices to the Temple in Jerusalem. Now we use the words of the siddur to connect with God.
- We used to live cloistered, separate lives from our non-Jewish neighbors. Now we are fully and happily integrated in an inclusive society (which of course presents other, unique issues).
- We used to have one way to worship. Now there are numerous movements and ways to affiliate with countless synagogues.
- Men and women were always treated differently. Now all Jews who wish can participate in fully egalitarian congregations.
- LGBTQ individuals had little or no place in mainstream Judaism. Now congregations (including those of the Conservative Movement) enthusiastically welcome same-sex couples and officiate at their marriages.

Why can't we add this to this list:

- All b'nei mitzvah kids were trained exactly the same way and their ceremonies were virtually identical. Now we meet each child where they are, deciding the best path and age for them to connect to Jewish adulthood. We prepare the whole child for a lifetime of Jewish connection.

In so many ways, we are truly living in a new golden age of Judaism. But each of these monumental changes came about because of disruption.

## Synagogues and Professionals

It would be too easy to read the last section and characterize those families and teens who wish to implement any measure of these changes as the sole disruptors. Taken this way, it would be tempting for Jewish professionals and their synagogues to view themselves as the ones being disrupted. That results in an adversarial model: *we* know what we're doing; we wish *they* would leave us alone and let us get to work.

Instead, these changes work well when students and teachers, families and Jewish professionals work in concert as a team. After all, even if our specific goals—see chapter 9—might be wildly different, every person involved in this process has the same overarching objective: to form a strong and mature connection to the Jewish community that will last and evolve over the course of a person's lifetime.

Given our common mission, here are some steps for Jewish institutions, professionals, and tutors to think about:

## 1. Invite
Having done this over the course of a long career, I work very hard to combat a sense of complacency—a Cantor-Knows-Best attitude. Someone following this pattern would not only dictate the procedure that all b'nei mitzvah kids must follow, but also inculcate the students with only the goals and objectives that *the professional* deems to be important. There would be no room for any other view but the established one.

- You must learn this haftarah.
- You will learn pages X through Y.
- It is most important that you learn how to lead (or how to look like you're leading) a Shabbat morning service.
- Being a Jewish adult means coming to services all the time.

Instead, begin the process of becoming b'nei mitzvah as the first steps of a journey taken together. Invite the family to share their vision and be open to a perspective that's different from the established norm. Earlier in my career, I contacted a family to inform them that it was time to begin lessons with their son. The parents let me know that they were going to hold off on a ceremony for the time being. I don't recall the exact reason (whether it was a family matter, a level of emotional maturity, or social issues), but my initial reaction was incredulity! It was inconceivable to me that someone could say, "Thank you; we need to hold off for now." I felt as though this family was making a grave error and not seeing the big picture clearly.

More recently, this has happened on other isolated occasions. Years of experience and a more rounded outlook have completely changed my perspective. Not only am I accepting of such a position, I applaud it. It can't be easy for a family to paddle against the strong current of convention and make a decision that they deem to be in their child's best interest. I make certain to support these families, remain a presence with them, and continue to elicit as much information as possible as to their reasons for postponing. Rather than having the synagogue shut a door to this type of family, the professionals need to invite them to participate in constructive dialogue. Yes, it may very well be the correct, appropriate, and proper decision to wait or to completely reimagine what this bar or bat mitzvah will look like. We won't know until we invite them to share their views with us.

## 2. Engage

This, of course, is the next natural step. Once you create an atmosphere of openness and acceptance to all families—meeting each one where they are—then synagogues must continue to engage all families throughout the process.

This is completely in keeping with the liberal arts model of a university that I suggested before. In college, each student, regardless of the particular track or course of study that they've decided is best, must keep in constant contact with their academic advisor. This serves to ensure that the student is on the right track as far as choosing courses or pursuing areas of study. But even more importantly, the advisor acts as a sounding board for any issues, questions, or obstacles that arise.

The importance of having an "academic advisor" in b'nei mitzvah training cannot be overstated. Finding new ways to mark this occasion and deciding how best to fulfill the goals that are most important are tasks that are best done together—with active and intellectually provocative conversations.

Seen in this light, the opposite of "engage" is "dictate," and unfortunately that describes much of the current state of b'nei mitzvah preparation and education. I suspect that some Jewish professionals who work in synagogues feel that it's a show of religious weakness or a lack of commitment to Jewish tradition if they bend, compromise, or capitulate to the wishes of individual families who express a desire for something different. It's the slippery slope argument and we've all seen it: if we give in to *them*, then *everyone* will be asking for what they want.

Imagine how exciting synagogue life would be if that actually happened.

## 3. Adapt

I wrote the same thing in the previous section for parents. Everyone in this process needs to adapt to change. Just as I posed a series of questions for parents and families, I'd like to pose a parallel set for those who work in Jewish institutions:

- As you take your first steps to really listen to and engage with b'nei mitzvah families, have you discovered any new insights about them that affects what you think might be best for their child?
- How do you see their child connecting to certain types of material?
- Do you think that this is the right age for this milestone? Is there any value in postponing? What age do you think would be best?

If cantors, rabbis, and other tutors asked these questions sincerely and openly and truly internalized the responses, we would *have* to adapt. There are so many varied answers to these questions, and one must acknowledge that there simply cannot be only one possible path that adequately represents what's best for every single individual. That makes this book more than a fascinating (or controversial) thought exercise. Instead, it becomes an imperative call to adapt our current course of study to meet the needs of our Jewish community. Just as families must adapt to a new way of thinking, so too must the institution.

### 4. Accept

Remember the example I gave earlier of the family that came to me many years ago and told me that they were unable to proceed with a bar mitzvah in the usual time frame. I simply don't recall their specific reasons, probably more because of a lack of listening on my part rather than their failure to communicate. At that time, I was not accepting of this viewpoint at all. I felt like I knew best and they were making a selfish and uninformed decision. If my primary role was to facilitate a path for this family and their child to connect—religiously and spiritually—to Judaism, then my insistence that they exclusively adhere to the synagogue's instructions was counterproductive.

By definition, meeting kids and families where they are means *accepting* them. Each family, each bar or bat mitzvah kid is an individual with a distinct set of needs and capacity for spiritual development. The sanctuary is not the exclusive domain of all things spiritual or religious. Even if they express a view that runs counter to our own thinking, if we then say, "I just cannot accept what you're saying or suggesting," then we can forget about anything that comes after. If goal #1 of becoming b'nei mitzvah is seeking to form the strongest possible connection to a lifetime of Jewish involvement (in whatever form that takes), then refusing to accept any alternate point of view is shutting the door on these families—probably forever.

## 5. Rejoice!

I've seen more b'nei mitzvah ceremonies over the years than I can count, and on numerous occasions I look around the room and see how everyone is reacting. More often than you'd expect, I see the parents and immediate family sitting there stone-faced—no smiles, no sense of enjoyment. They are figuratively gritting their teeth to endure the entire ordeal (and presumably to get to their party where the actual fun will take place).

This makes me wonder: Can we really blame these people? This is on us. We've taken some Jewish family that has placed all of their trust in us.

- They trust that we know what's truly best for their child.
- They trust that we know the one way to provide a Jewish education.
- They trust that the preparation we provide for their child's bar or bat mitzvah is authentic and complete.
- They trust that if they follow all the rules—attend Religious School and all lessons—then their child will properly develop an adult relationship and connection to Judaism.
- They trust that sitting in the sanctuary and attending services—all the more so when we set requirements for them to be there—will result in a heightened sense of religious spirituality.

And then we act surprised when they are present at what is supposed to be the grand culmination of their kid's short lifetime of learning but sense, accurately, that something is missing. These parents are typically witnessing an incredible performance, but are underwhelmed when they realize that there hasn't been much growth.

But when parents, kids, and Jewish professionals all work together to reimagine what they would like to see happen—that truly becomes an opportunity to rejoice. Whether after a course of learning that spans months or years, whether the student is thirteen or sixteen, whether the event takes place within the walls of the sanctuary or in a family's living room—this is a call to create a true opportunity to rejoice over the way that one individual has chosen to demonstrate their nascent adult connection to the Jewish people.

Reimagine. Rethink. Rejoice.

The only limits are those that we place upon ourselves.

~

# One Last Word

Back in the introduction I wrote that I wanted to begin a conversation. Hopefully, over the past thirteen chapters you've considered what I've written in that light. This book was never meant to be a manual—or a definitive how-to volume on the way that we can take some supposedly meaningless event and infuse it with a new life and updated significance. If I can continue the metaphor of b'nei mitzvah as representing a journey that one takes, then this book is less of a road map, showing every possible route, and more of a travel guide, pointing out some possible destinations and inspiring you to explore on your own.

Our current b'nei mitzvah system of preparation, learning, and celebrating can indeed be a meaningful one. I am not saying that it is bereft of any aspect of spirituality or relevance or that no one other than myself has ever suggested making changes or initiated creative innovations. But in many cases, the b'nei mitzvah process is missing aspects that could be of enormous benefit to individual kids, their families, and the Jewish clergy and professionals who live and breathe our tradition each day and want nothing more than to pass along a priceless and enduring legacy to the next generations.

We don't need to settle. Yes, we have something good. But by participating in this conversation with each other and with our students, children, and congregants, we can reimagine how the next generation of b'nei mitzvah have the potential to be spectacular. We would truly be participating together in Raising the Bar Mitzvah.

# Resources for Learning More

## Books

*The Mitzvah Project Book: Making Mitzvah Part of Your Bar/Bat Mitzvah . . . and Your Life*, by Diane Heiman and Liz Suneby

*The Out of the Box Bat Mitzvah: A Guide to Creating a Meaningful Milestone*, by Esther Goldenberg

*Reclaiming Bar/Bat Mitzvah as a Spiritual Rite of Passage*, by Rabbi Goldie Milgram and Taylor Rozek

*Putting God on the Guest List: How to Reclaim the Spiritual Meaning of Your Child's Bar or Bat Mitzvah*, by Rabbi Jeffrey K. Salkin

*Bar Mitzvah, a History*, by Rabbi Michael Hilton

*Bar Mitzvah: A Guide to Spiritual Growth*, by Marc-Alain Ouaknin

*Bar Mitzvah, Bat Mitzvah: The Ceremony, the Party, and How the Day Came to Be*, by Bert Metter

## Website

Lab/Shul: https://labshul.org/raising-the-bar-b-mitzvah/

## Articles

"Alternative Bar and Bat Mitzvah Ceremonies," by My Jewish Learning, https://www.myjewishlearning.com/article/alternative-bar-and-bat-mitzvah-ceremonies/.

"It's Time to Raise the Bar on the Bar/Bat Mitzvah," by Rabbi Joel E. Hoffman, https://
www.stljewishlight.com/opinion/commentaries/it-s-time-to-raise-the-bar-on
-the-bar/article_45492cee-229c-11e6-86c3-3399690de494.html

## Podcast

@13, by Moving Traditions, https://www.movingtraditions.org/category/podcast/

# Index

# About the Author

Cantor Matt Axelrod is the author of *Surviving Your Bar/Bat Mitzvah: The Ultimate Insider's Guide* and *Your Guide to the Jewish Holidays: From Shofar to Seder*, and has been a regular columnist and contributor to the online Bar & Bat Mitzvah Guide. He has been a frequent presenter at synagogues, Jewish community centers, and conferences to speak to groups of parents and teens about the process of preparing for their B'nei Mitzvah and how to successfully navigate that period. Cantor Axelrod is a past member of the United Synagogue Commission on Jewish Education and currently serves as a national officer of the Cantors Assembly.